The Get Ready Guide for The Bergen Academies Adm

Second Edition Published 2011   First Edition Published 2009

Copying or distributing any part of this book in any manner without the written permission of the author is not allowed.

Disclaimer: The Bergen Academies are not involved in the writing of this book.

Please send all inquiries to:

Kareem Gouda

kareem@kareemgouda.com

201-793-7345

This Book

This book contains all the math topics and essay writing rules and useful tricks for the essay that you need to know to ace The Bergen Academies Admission Test. After the 12 chapters you will find a practice sheet with questions that are very similar to those published by the Bergen Academies; these questions are explained in details. After this practice sheet you will find a full length exam that is again very similar in level and format to the test you will see on test day. Finally, there are over 2000 practice questions on the basic concepts presented in each math chapter in the book. I'm sure that you will feel confident on test day after reading this book and answering all its practice questions. You will also find free extra practice on our website **www.SKOOLOO.com** as well as videos that support this book and offer many helpful tricks and shortcuts.

Every effort has been made to review and *re-review* the contents of the book, but it is definitely not flawless. Please send me an email and tell me if you find any errors (and do tell me what the errors are).

Also, please send me an email at kareem@kareemgouda.com to learn the details of our live and video courses that cover the practice problems and tests released by the Bergen Academies.

I wish you the best of luck in entering The Academies and beyond.

TABLE OF CONTENTS

PART ONE

CHAPTER 1 THE BASIC STUFF	1
CHAPTER 2 FRACTIONS	24
CHAPTER 3 DECIMALS	39
CHAPTER 4 RATIO & PROPORTION	49
CHAPTER 5 PERCENTS	53
CHAPTER 6 STATISTICS	64
CHAPTER 7 PROBABILITY	68
CHAPTER 8 SEQUENCES	72
CHAPTER 9 BASIC ALGEBRA & WORD PROBLEMS	77
CHAPTER 10 GEOMETRY	86
CHAPTER 11 SEE YOU LATER CALCULATOR	97
CHAPTER 12 THE ESSAY	101

PART TWO PRACTICE

BCA PRACTICE SHEET WITH DETAILED ANSWERS	131
FULL LENGTH BCA PRACTICE TEST	148
BASIC CONCEPTS MATH PRACTICE	153

1. The Basic Stuff

1. Types of Numbers
2. Place Value
3. Expanded Form
4. Ordering Numbers
5. Rounding Whole Numbers
6. Divisibility Tests
7. Commutative Property
8. Associative Property
9. Distributive Property
10. Adding & Subtracting Zero
11. Multiplying & Dividing by Zero
12. Multiplying & Dividing by One
13. Factors of a Number
14. Prime Factorization
15. Multiples of a Number
16. Exponents
17. Square Roots (Radicals)
18. Factorial Notation
19. Order of Operations
20. The Number Line
21. The Absolute Value
22. Adding & Subtracting with Negative Numbers
23. Multiplying & Dividing with Negative Numbers
24. Coordinates on a Grid

1. Types of Numbers

Classification of numbers and their names can be a bit confusing. So I'll just list the four most important types of numbers and four notes to go along with them.

. *Real Numbers* are pretty much any type of number including negatives, fractions, and decimals.

. *Whole numbers* are the counting numbers (1,2,3..) and zero like 0, 1, 2, 3, 4, 5, 6

. *Integers* are negative and positive whole numbers as well as zero like -3,-2,-1, 0, 1, 2, 3, 4, 5….

. *A Prime number* is a number that is divisible by only two numbers, 1 and itself. For example
  7 is a prime number because it is only divisible by 1 and 7.

Notes:

. The number 1 is not a prime number (because it is not divisible by two numbers).

. The number 2 is the only even prime number.

. The number 0 is neither positive nor negative.

. The number 0 is an even number.

Examples	Type of Numbers
-2, -1.5, 0, 1, 2, 2.75, 7/2	Real Numbers
0, 1, 2, 3, 4, 5	Whole Numbers
-5, -4, -3, -2, -1, 0, 1, 2, 3, 4, 5	Integers
2,3,5,7,11	Prime Numbers

2. Place Value

The position, or *place*, of a digit in a number determines the actual value the digit represents. This table shows the place value for various positions:

Place (underlined)	Name of Position
1 00<u>0</u>	Ones (units) position
1 0<u>0</u>0	Tens
1 <u>0</u>00	Hundreds
<u>1</u> 000	Thousands
1 0<u>0</u>0 000	Ten thousands
1 <u>0</u>00 000	Hundred Thousands

Example:
The number 521040 has a 5 in the hundred thousands place, a 2 in the ten thousands place, a 1 in the thousands place, a 0 in the hundreds place, a 4 in the tens place, and a 0 in the ones place.

3. Expanded Form

The expanded form of a number is the sum of the values of each digit of that number.

Example:

9436 = 9000 + 400 + 30 + 6.
So **9436** equals
9 thousand (thousands place) + **4** hundred (hundreds place) + **3** tens (tens place) + **6** ones (ones place)

4. Ordering

Symbols are used to show how the size of one number compares to another. These symbols are:

$<$: less than

$>$: greater than

$=$: equals

$\geq$: greater than or equal

$\leq$: less than or equal

For example:

2 is *less* than 4 so we can write: **2 < 4**.
4 is *greater* than 2 so we can write: **4 > 2**.
The number of days in a month is *greater than or equal* to 28 so we write **Days of Month $\geq$ 28**

The number of days in a month is *less than or equal* to 31 so we write **Days of Month $\leq$ 31**

5. Rounding Whole Numbers

To round to the nearest *something* means to find the closest number having all zeros to the right of that *something's* place. That *something* either stays as it is or increases by one.

Now, let's use actual numbers not *somethings* to make this a bit easier. Read along.

To round **137** to the nearest *tens* means to find the closest number having all zeros to the right of **3** (*the tens place*). That means that the **3** should either stay as it is (**3**) or increase by one (becomes **4**).

So, should it be **130** or **140** ?
Since the ones place has a **7** then we should round up making the answer **140.**

When the digit 5, 6, 7, 8, or 9 appears in the ones place, round up; when the digit 0, 1, 2, 3, or 4 appears in the ones place, round down.

So if we're rounding to the nearest hundreds: the hundreds place will either stay as it is or increase by one, depending on the digit after the hundreds place (tens), while all the numbers to the right of the hundreds place (tens and units) become zeros. That means that rounding 1534 to the nearest hundreds gives 1500. Because the digit after the 5 (hundreds) is 3 (tens) so we round down to 1500.

Examples:
Rounding **118** to the nearest **ten** gives **120**.
Rounding **155** to the nearest **ten** gives **160**.
Rounding **502** to the nearest **ten** gives **500**.
Rounding **180** to the nearest **hundred** gives **200**.
Rounding **150090** to the nearest **hundred thousand** gives **200000**.
Rounding **1234** to the nearest **thousand** gives **1000**.

We can also find the estimate of a sum of numbers using rounding

Example:
To estimate the sum 119260 + 700 to the nearest thousand, first round each number in the sum, resulting in a new sum of 119000 + 1000. Then add to get the estimate of 120000.

6. Divisibility Tests

There are many quick ways of telling whether or not a whole number is divisible by certain basic whole numbers. These can be useful tricks, especially for large numbers.

Divisibility by 2
A whole number is divisible by 2 if the digit in its units position is even, (either 0, 2, 4, 6, or 8).

Examples:
The number 74 is divisible by 2 since the digit in the units position is 4, which is even.
The number 335836 is divisible by 2 since the digit in the units position is 6, which is even.
The number 1358000 is divisible by 2 since the digit in the units position is 0, which is even.

Divisibility by 3
A whole number is divisible by 3 if the sum of all its digits is divisible by 3.

Examples:
The number 267 is divisible by three, since the sum of its digits is 15, which is divisible by 3.
The number 872151 is divisible by three, since the sum of its digits is 24, which is divisible by 3.

Divisibility by 4
A whole number is divisible by 4 if the number formed by the last two digits is divisible by 4.

Examples:
The number 3524 is divisible by 4 since the number formed by its last two digits, 24, is divisible by 4.
The number 1368336 is divisible by 4 since **36**, is divisible by 4.

Divisibility by 5
A whole number is divisible by 5 if the digit in its units position is 0 or 5.

Examples:
The number 95 is divisible by 5 since the last digit is 5.
The number 358370 is divisible by 5 since the last digit is 0.

Divisibility by 6
A number is divisible by 6 if it is divisible by 2 **and** divisible by 3. We can use each of the divisibility tests to check if a number is divisible by 6: *its units digit is even* (divisible by 2) and *the sum of its digits is divisible by 3*.

Examples:
The number 714468 is divisible by 6, since its units digit is even, and the sum of its digits is 30, which is divisible by 3.
The number 298563 is **not divisible** by 6, since its units digit is not even.
The number 376942 is **not divisible** by 6, since it is not divisible by 3. The sum of its digits is 31, which is not divisible by 3, so the number 367942 is not divisible by 3.

Divisibility by 8
A whole number is divisible by 8 if the number formed by the last three digits is divisible by 8.

Example:
The number 8215**160** is divisible by 8 since **160** is divisible by 8.

Divisibility by 9
A whole number is divisible by 9 if the sum of all its digits is divisible by 9.

Example:
The number 1377 is divisible by nine, since the sum of its digits is 18, which is divisible by 9.

Divisibility by 10
A whole number is divisible by 10 if the digit in its units position is 0.

Example:
The number 1229570 is divisible by 10 since the last digit is 0.

7. Commutative Property

Addition and Multiplication are commutative. That means that switching the order of the numbers being added or multiplied does not change the result.

Examples:

$105 + 8 = 8 + 105$
$100 \times 7 = 7 \times 100$
$15 \times 7 \times 25 = 25 \times 15 \times 7$

---

8. Associative Property

Addition and multiplication are associative. That means that the order that numbers are grouped in addition and multiplication does not affect the result.

Examples:

$(3 + 10) + 6 = 3 + (10 + 6) = 19$
$2 \times (10 \times 7) = (2 \times 10) \times 7 = 140$

---

9. Distributive Property

The distributive property of multiplication over addition and subtraction means that multiplication may be distributed over addition and subtraction. What?
Look at the examples, I'm sure you'll understand.

Examples:

$10 \times (40 + 3) = (10 \times 40) + (10 \times 3)$ *[both the left and right hand sides equal 430]*

$3 \times (12 - 78) = (3 \times 12) - (3 \times 78)$ *[both the left and right hand sides equal -198]*

10. Adding & Subtracting Zero

Adding or subtracting 0 to a number leaves it unchanged.

Example:

$78 + 0 = 78$
$78 - 0 = 78$

11. Multiplying & Dividing by Zero

Multiplying any number by 0 gives 0.

Examples:

$85 \times 0 = 0$
$1253 \times 0 = 0$

Note:

Dividing a number by zero is undefined, which means there's no such thing as divided by zero

Zero divided by any number equals zero.

Examples:

$5 \div 0 =$ Undefined, makes no sense, no answer…..

$0 \div 5 = 0$.

12. Multiplying & Dividing by One

We call 1 the multiplicative identity. Multiplying any number by 1 leaves the number unchanged. Also dividing any number by 1 leaves the number unchanged.

Example:

$54 \times 1 = 54$

$548 \div 1 = 548$

Quick Quiz:

Do you know what *1 ÷ by a number* (or 1 / a number) is called?

It's called the reciprocal of the number. So 1/7 is the reciprocal of 7.

13. Factors of a Number

You can find the factors of a number by checking what number pairs (two numbers multiplied by each other) make up this number. Look at the following example.

What are the factors of 12?

1 x 12 = 12
2 x 6 = 12
3 x 4 = 12

So the factors of 12 are 1, 2, 3, 4, 6 & 12.

We did not put 4 x 3 = 12, 6 x 2 = 12, and 12 x 1 = 12 because they are the same as 1 x 12 = 12, 2 x 6 = 12, and 3 x 4 = 12 which we already put.

We did not write 5 x Anything because 12 is not divisible by 5.

Always remember that 1 and the number itself (12 in the previous example) are factors of the number.

Here's another example:
What are the factors of 35?

1 x 35 = 35
5 x 7 = 35

So the factors of 35 are 1, 5, 7, and 35
Note that we did not repeat 35 x 1 or 7 x 5. We also didn't use 2, 3, and 4 because 35 is not divisible by either of them.

14. Prime Factorization

"Prime Factorization" is finding **which prime numbers** you need to multiply together to get the original number.

We do that by dividing the number by the smallest possible prime number (remember: 1 is not a prime number) then if the answer isn't a prime number, we divide that answer by another prime number and so on till the last number is a prime number. Then simply list all the prime numbers you've written (*the ones you divided by* and *the answers you got*). These are your prime factors.

To check your work, multiply the prime numbers by each other; you should get the original number that you were factorizing.
Confusing? Look at the examples.

Example 1:

What are the prime factors of 12?

Let's start working from the smallest prime number, which is 2, so let's check:

$$12 \div 2 = 6$$

But 6 is not a prime number, so we need to factor it further:
$$6 \div 2 = 3$$
And 3 **is** a prime number, so we're done:
$$12 = 2 \times 2 \times 3$$

So 2, 2, and 3 are the prime factors of 12.
As you can see, every **factor** is a **prime number**, so the answer must be right.

The prime factorization of 12 is $2 \times 2 \times 3$, which can also be written as $2^2 \times 3$.

Example 2:

What is the prime factorization of 147?

Can we divide 147 evenly by 2? No, so we should try the next prime number, 3:
$$147 \div 3 = 49$$
Then we try factoring 49, and find that 7 is the smallest prime number that works:
$$49 \div 7 = 7$$
And that is as far as we need to go, because all the factors are prime numbers.
The prime factorization of $147 = 3 \times 7 \times 7$

15. Multiples of a Number

You can find the multiples of a number by multiplying that number by 1, 2, 3, 4, 5, and so on.

<u>What are the multiples of 12?</u>

1 x 12 = 12
2 x 12 = 24
3 x 12 = 36
4 x 12 = 48
5 x 12 = 60
And so on…

So 12, 24, 36, 48, 60,… are multiples of 12.

16. Exponents (Powers of 2, 3, 4, ...)

Numbers with exponents look like this 5^6

The number being multiplied is called the base (5), and the exponent (6) tells how many times the base is multiplied by itself.

This means that 5 will be multiplied by itself 6 times

So 5^6 = 5x5x5x5x5x5 = 15625

Example:

4 ×4 ×4 ×4 ×4 ×4 = 4^6

The base in this example is 4, the exponent is 6.

We refer to this as four to the sixth power, or four to the power of six.

Examples:

2 ×2 ×2 = 2^3 = 8

23^1 = 23

1.3^2 = 1.3 × 1.3 = 1.69

0.5^3 = 0.5 × 0.5 × 0.5 = 0.125

10^7 = 10 × 10 × 10 × 10 × 10 × 10 × 10 = 10000000
When the base is 10 the answer is just a "1" with a number of zeros equal to the exponent (7 in the previous example)

Special Names:

A number with an exponent of two is referred to as the *square of a number*.

The square of a whole number is known as a *perfect square*. The numbers 1, 4, 9, 16, and 25 are all perfect squares.

A number with an exponent of three is referred to as the *cube of a number*.

The cube of a whole number is known as a *perfect cube*. The numbers 1, 8, 27, 64, and 125 are all perfect cubes.

Basic Rules of Exponents:

1. Add the exponents when multiplying equal bases.

Example:
$$3^2 \times 3^3 = 3^{2+3} = 3^5$$

2. Subtract the exponents when dividing equal bases.

Example:
$$4^6 \div 4^4 = 4^{6-4} = 4^2$$

17. Square Roots (Radicals)

Roots (or radicals) are the "opposite" operation of applying exponents; you can "undo" a power with a radical.

For example, if you square 2, you get 4 (2 x 2), and if you "take the square root of 4", you get 2

Similarly, if you square 3, you get 9 (3 x 3), and if you "take the square root of 9", you get 3

2^2 = 4, so $\sqrt{4} = 2$

3^2 = 9, so $\sqrt{9} = 3$

Examples:

The square root of 9 is 3, since 3 × 3 = 9.

The square root of 289 is 17, since 17 × 17 = 289.

$\sqrt{400} = \sqrt{20 \times 20} = 20$

$\sqrt{16} = \sqrt{4 \times 4} = 4$

NOTE:

Multiplied values or divided values under a root can be rewritten as two roots.

Examples:

$\sqrt{9 \times 16}$ is the same as $\sqrt{9} \times \sqrt{16}$

$\sqrt{25 \div 4}$ is the same as $\sqrt{25} \div \sqrt{4}$

18. Factorial Notation $n!$

The product of the first *n* whole numbers starting with 1 and ending with **n** is written as $n!$

$n! = 1 \times 2 \times 3 \times 4 \times \ldots \times (n-1) \times n.$

Examples:

$4! = 1 \times 2 \times 3 \times 4 = 24$
$10! = 1 \times 2 \times 3 \times 4 \times 5 \times 6 \times 7 \times 8 \times 9 \times 10 = 3628800$

Tricks:

When dividing factorials, note that many of the numbers cancel out!

$$5! \div 4! = \frac{5!}{4!} = \frac{5 \times 4 \times 3 \times 2 \times 1}{4 \times 3 \times 2 \times 1} = 5$$

NOTE:

As a special case **0!** is equal to 1.

19. Order of Operations

Problem: Evaluate the following arithmetic expression:
3 + 5 x 2

Solution:

Student 1	Student 2
3 + 5 x 2	3 + 5 x 2
= 8 x 2	= 3 + 10
= 16	= 13

Each student interpreted the problem differently, resulting in two different answers. Student 1 performed the operation of addition first, then multiplication; whereas student 2 performed multiplication first, then addition. Student 2 was correct but student 1 was wrong.

So what should *you* do?

Use the Order of Operations Steps (in the following order of course):

1) Perform operations within **Parentheses**.
2) Perform operations with **Exponents.**
3) **Multiply** and **Divide**, whichever comes first, from left to right.
4) **Add** and **Subtract**, whichever comes first, from left to right.

Remember them as **P E M D A S**.

Example:

$1 + 20 \times 3^2 \div (7-2) =$

$1 + 20 \times 3^2 \div 5 =$ (we solved the parentheses: 7-2 =5)

$1 + 20 \times 9 \div 5 =$ (we solved the exponent: $3^2 = 9$)

$1 + 180 \div 5 =$ (we solved the multiplication: 20 X 9 =180)

$1 + 36 =$ (we solved the division: 180 ÷ 5 = 36)

37   (we solved the addition: 1+36 = 37)

20. The Number Line

The number line is a line labeled with numbers in increasing order from left to right, that extends in both directions:

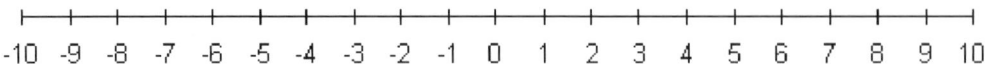

For any two different places on the number line, **the integer on the right is greater than the integer on the left**.

Examples:

9 > 4
6 > -9
-2 > -8
0 > -5

---

21. The Absolute Value

The **absolute value** of a number is always **the positive** form of that number (or zero if the number was originally zero). The absolute value of a number resembles the number of units a number is from zero on the number line regardless of it being positive or negative. That means that if a boy loses 5 pounds (-5) or gains 5 pounds (+5), the **absolute value** of his change in weight is **+5** pounds whether he lost or gained 5 pounds. We specify the absolute value of a number n by writing n in between two vertical bars: $|n|$. Remember that if a number is written without a + or – sign before it then that means it is positive (5 is the same as +5).

Examples:

|7| = 7
|-15| = 15
|0| = 0
|1234| = 1234
|-1234| = 1234
|-15.6| = 15.6
|3.04| = 3.04

22. Adding & Subtracting with Positive and Negative Numbers

When adding and subtracting positive & negative numbers follow the following rules:

* If the signs (+ or -) are the same.

Then the answer will be **the sum of the absolute values** of the numbers (Remember: that means the positive values of the numbers) and will have **the same sign** as the numbers being added or subtracted.

Examples:

5 + 2 = 7
(When a number does not have a sign before it that means it's positive, so 7 is the same as +7)

-5 – 2 = -7
(The sum of 5 & 2 which are the absolute values of -5 & -2 is 7. Then we add a negative sign)

* If the signs (+ or -) are different.

Then the answer will be **the bigger number minus the smaller number** (regardless of their signs) and will have **the same sign as the bigger number**.

5 – 2 = 3 (the answer 3 is positive just like the bigger number, 5)

2 – 5 = -3 (the answer 3 is negative just like the bigger number, 5).

Be careful: We are comparing the values regardless of the signs. That's why I said, in the previous example, that 5 is bigger than 2. I didn't say that -5 is bigger than 2; that would be wrong.

23. Multiplying & Dividing with Positive and Negative Numbers

To multiply or divide positive and negative numbers, always multiply or divide the absolute values (remember: this means that we will only deal with the positive value of the number) and then use the following rules to determine the sign of the answer.

When you multiply two integers with the **same signs**, the result is always **positive**. Just multiply the absolute values and make the answer positive.

Positive x positive = positive

5 x 4 = 20

Negative x negative = positive

-5 x -4 = 20

When you multiply two integers with **different signs**, the result is always **negative**. Just multiply the absolute values and make the answer negative.

Positive x negative = negative

5 x -4 = -20

Negative x positive = negative

-5 x 4 = -20

When you divide two integers with the **same signs**, the result is always **positive**. Just divide the absolute values and make the answer positive.

Positive ÷ positive = positive

10 ÷ 2 = 5

Negative ÷ negative = positive

-10 ÷ -2 = 5

When you divide two integers with **different signs**, the result is always **negative**. Just divide the absolute values and make the answer negative.

Positive ÷ negative = negative

10 ÷ -2 = -5

Negative ÷ positive = negative

-10 ÷ 2 = - 5

Important Note:

You should never leave 2 signs (+ or -) next to each other without a number in between. This rule is so important that I'll write it again:
You should never leave 2 signs (+ or -) next to each other without a number in between

So, what should you do? Use the following rules:

+ + = + Example 3 + (+5) = 3 + 5

- - = + Example 3 - (-5) = 3 + 5

+ - = - Example 3 + (-5) = 3 - 5

- + = - Example 3 - (+5) = 3 - 5

Let's try something longer:

5 + (-3) + (-2) - (-5) =

5 - 3 - 2 + 5 = 5

24. Coordinates on A Grid

Think of a grid as two number lines. One is horizontal just like a normal number line; that is called the X - Axis. The other is vertical and is called the Y – Axis.

Any point on the grid will have 2 coordinates, an X coordinate (which is the point's X value) and a Y coordinate (which is the point's Y value). Therefore any point can be written as (x , y). The origin (the point of intersection of the X & Y axes) has coordinates (0 , 0).

Example:

The origin below is where the x-axis and the y-axis meet. The origin has coordinates of (0,0). Point A has coordinates (3,4), since it is 3 units to the right and 4 units up from the origin. Point B has coordinates (1,2), since it is 1 unit to the right, and 2 units up from the origin. Point C has coordinates (-4,1), since it is 4 units to the left, and 1 unit up from the origin. Point D has coordinates (-4,-3), since it is 4 units to the left, and 3 units down from the origin. Point E has coordinates (6,-2), since it is 6 units to the right, and 2 units down from the origin.

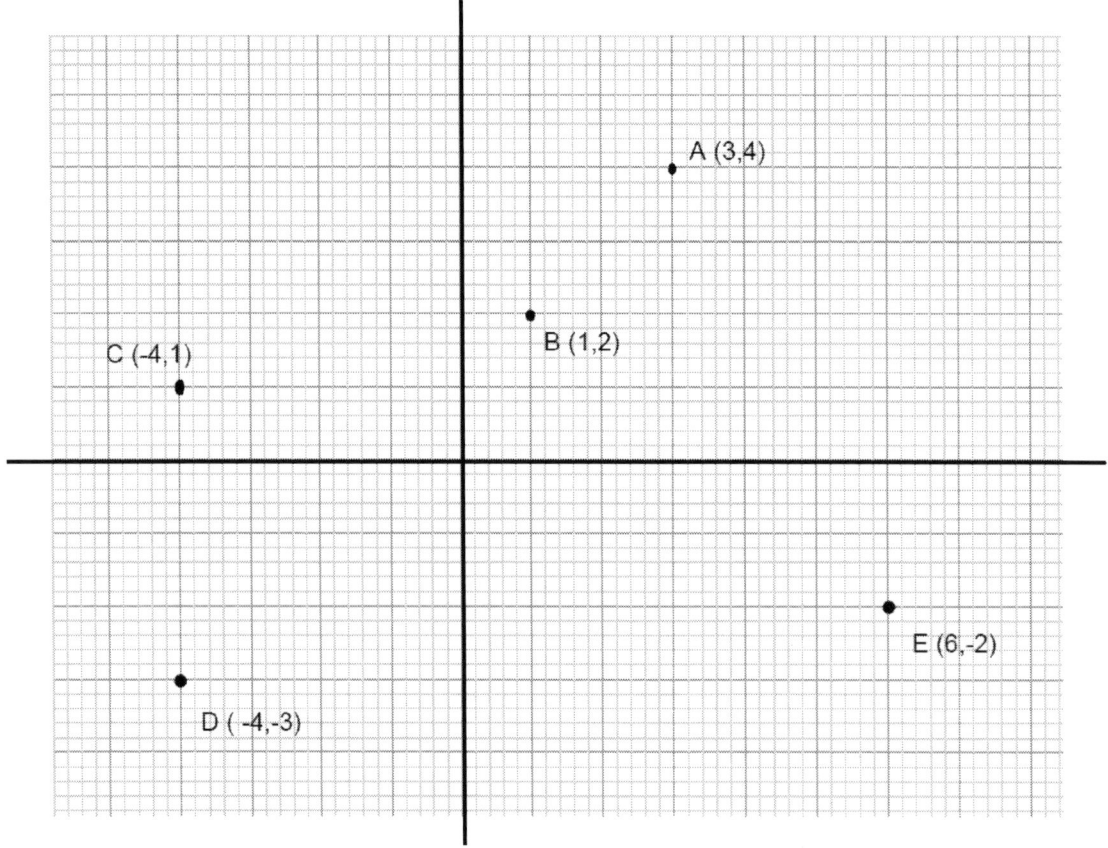

2. Fractions

1. What is a Fraction?

2. Improper Fractions

3. Mixed Numbers

4. Comparing Fractions

5. Greatest Common Factor (Sometimes called the Greatest Common Divisor)

6. Least Common Multiple (Sometimes called the Lowest Common Denominator)

7. Multiplying or Dividing the Numerator & Denominator by the Same Number

8. The Simplest Form of a Fraction (Also called The Lowest Term)

9. Reciprocal

10. Converting Mixed Numbers to Improper Fractions

11. Converting Improper Fractions to Mixed Numbers

12. Converting a Fraction to a Decimal

13. Adding and Subtracting Fractions

14. Adding and Subtracting Mixed Numbers

15. Multiplying Fractions and Fractions

16. Multiplying Fractions and Whole Numbers

17. Multiplying Mixed Numbers

18. Dividing Fractions

19. Simplifying Complex Fraction

1. What is a Fraction?

A fraction is a number that expresses part of a group.

Fractions are written in the form $\frac{a}{b}$, where a and b are whole numbers, and the number b is not 0.

Why can't "b" be zero?

Remember: there is no such thing as a number divided by zero hence there is no such thing as a number over zero.

The number a is called the **numerator**, and the number b is called the **denominator**.

Example:

The following numbers are all fractions

$$\frac{3}{4}, \frac{1}{2}, \frac{4}{99}$$

Example:

The fraction $\frac{3}{4}$ represents the shaded portion of the circle below. There are 4 pieces in the group, and 3 of them are shaded.

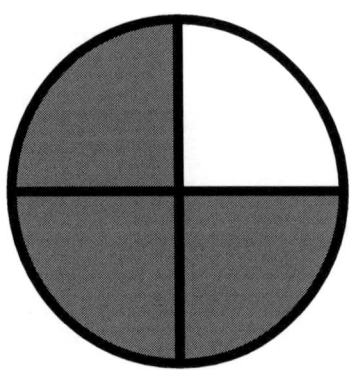

2. Improper Fractions

Improper fractions have numerators that are larger than or equal to their denominators.

Examples:

$\frac{11}{4}$, $\frac{5}{5}$, and $\frac{13}{3}$ are improper fractions.

---

3. Mixed Numbers

Mixed numbers have a whole number part and a fraction part.

Examples:

$2\frac{3}{4}$ and $6\frac{1}{2}$ are mixed numbers.

This means that $2\frac{3}{4}$ is equal **to 2** and $\frac{3}{4}$, which is $2 + \frac{3}{4}$.

4. Comparing Fractions

1. To compare fractions with the same denominator, look at their numerators.

The larger fraction is the one with the larger numerator.

Example: $\frac{3}{4}$ is greater than $\frac{1}{4}$ because **3** is greater than **1** (the denominator is the same in both)

2. To compare fractions with the same numerator, look at their denominators.

The larger fraction is the one with the smaller denominator.

Example: $\frac{3}{7}$ is greater than $\frac{3}{8}$ because **7** is smaller than **8** (the numerator is the same in both)

3. To compare fractions with different denominators, take the cross products.

The **first cross-product** is the **product of the first numerator** (on the left) **and the second denominator** (on the right).
The **second cross-product** is the product of the **second numerator** (on the right) and **the first denominator** (on the left).

Then compare the cross products using the following rules:

a. If the cross-products are equal, the fractions are equal. They are called **equivalent fractions**.
b. If the first cross product is larger, the first fraction is larger.
c. If the second cross product is larger, the second fraction is larger.

Example:

Compare the fractions $\frac{3}{7}$ and $\frac{1}{2}$.

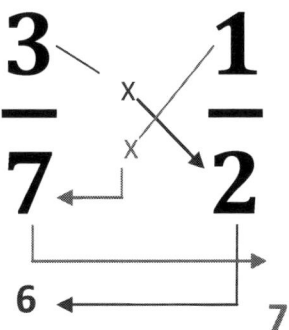

We put the **first cross-product (3 × 2 = 6) under the first fraction**.
We put the **second cross-product (1 × 7 = 7) under the second fraction**.

Now compare both cross-products, since 7 is bigger than 6 then $\frac{1}{2} > \frac{3}{7}$

**Make sure you put the cross-products in their proper places. If you mix them up, you'll
get a wrong answer.**

Example:
Compare the fractions $\frac{13}{20}$ and $\frac{3}{5}$.

The first cross-product is the product of the first numerator and the second denominator:

13 × 5 = 65.

The second cross-product is the product of the second numerator and the first denominator:

3 × 20 = 60.

Since the first cross-product is larger, the first fraction is larger.

5. Greatest Common Factor (Sometimes called the Greatest Common Divisor)

Remember how we used to find the factors of a number in chapter one?

To find the greatest common factor of two or more whole numbers, we list the factors of these numbers and then find the **common** factors. The **greatest** of theses **common factors** is our greatest common factor (just as the name suggests).

Example: *What is the greatest common factor of 36 and 54?*

List the factors of 36 & 54:

36: 1, 2, 3, 4, 6, 9, 12, 18, 36

54: 1, 2, 3, 6, 9, 18, 27, 54

The common factors are: 1, 2, 3, 6, 9, and 18. The greatest common factor is: 18.

---

6. Least Common Multiple (Sometimes called the Lowest Common Denominator)

Remember how we used to find the multiples of a number in chapter one?

To find the least common multiple of two or more whole numbers, we list the multiples of these numbers and then find the **common** multiples. The **least** of theses **common multiples** is our least common multiple (just as the name suggests).

Example: *Find the least common multiple of 12 and 42.*

List the multiples of each number, and look for the smallest number that appears in both lists.

12: 12, 24, 36, 48, 60, 72, 84, ...

42: 42, 84, 126, 168, 210, ...

We see that the number 84 is the smallest number that appears in each list.

TRICK:

Always start by finding the multiples of the bigger number. You see, the least common multiple can't be the first three multiples of 12 which are 12, 24, or 36 because they are smaller than 42, which is the first multiple of 42. This means that the first possible common multiple of 12 & 42 can only be 42 or bigger.

---

7. Multiplying or Dividing the Numerator & Denominator by the Same Number

* For any fraction, multiplying the numerator and denominator by the same nonzero number gives an equivalent fraction. We can convert one fraction to an equivalent fraction by using this method.

Examples:

$$\frac{3}{4} = \frac{3 \times 2}{4 \times 2} = \frac{6}{8} \qquad (\frac{3}{4} \text{ and } \frac{6}{8} \text{ are equal})$$

$$\frac{1}{2} = \frac{1 \times 3}{2 \times 3} = \frac{3}{6} \qquad (\frac{1}{2} \text{ and } \frac{3}{6} \text{ are equal})$$

* For any fraction, dividing the numerator and denominator by the same nonzero number gives an equivalent fraction. We can convert one fraction to an equivalent fraction by using this method.

Examples:

$$\frac{6}{8} = \frac{6 \div 2}{8 \div 2} = \frac{3}{4} \qquad (\frac{6}{8} \text{ and } \frac{3}{4} \text{ are equal})$$

$$\frac{3}{6} = \frac{3 \div 3}{6 \div 3} = \frac{1}{2} \qquad (\frac{3}{6} \text{ and } \frac{1}{2} \text{ are equal})$$

You see, in all the examples above:

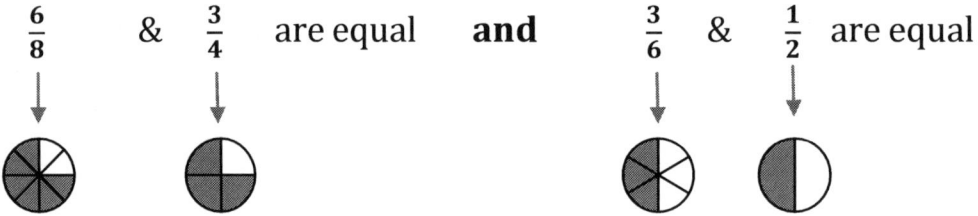

$\frac{6}{8}$ & $\frac{3}{4}$ are equal **and** $\frac{3}{6}$ & $\frac{1}{2}$ are equal

---

8. The Simplest Form of a Fraction (Also called The Lowest Term)

A fraction is in its simplest form or in its lowest terms when the only common factor of its numerator and denominator is 1. To find the simplest form of a fraction:

Divide the numerator and denominator by their greatest common factor.

$\frac{6}{4} = \frac{6 \div 2}{4 \div 2} = \frac{3}{2}$ (we divided by 2 because 2 is the greatest common factor of 6 & 4)

$\frac{7}{49} = \frac{7 \div 7}{49 \div 7} = \frac{1}{7}$ (we divided by 7 because 7 is the greatest common factor of 7 & 49)

---

9. Reciprocal

The reciprocal of any number is 1 divided by that number; however, in fractions, 1 divided by a fraction is just the fraction with numerator and denominator switched.

The reciprocal of a fraction is obtained by switching its numerator and denominator.

Example:

The reciprocal of $\frac{23}{4}$ is $\frac{4}{23}$

10. Converting Mixed Numbers to Improper Fractions

To change a mixed number into an improper fraction, multiply the whole number by the denominator then add that product (whole number X denominator) to the numerator of the fraction part. The result is the new numerator. The original denominator does not change.

Examples:

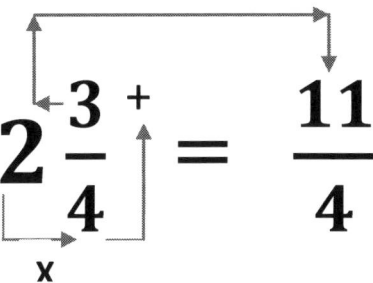

---

11. Converting Improper Fractions to Mixed Numbers

To change an improper fraction into a mixed number, divide the numerator by the denominator. The result is the whole number and the remainder is the numerator of the fractional part. The denominator does not change.

Examples:

$\frac{11}{4} = 11 \div 4 = 2$ *remainder* **3.** Which means **2 & three over four** OR $2\frac{3}{4}$

Another way to do this is to write the numerator (11) as two numbers plus each other so that the first number is the biggest possible number divisible by the denominator (4).

Then rewrite the fraction as two fractions plus each other, the first fraction becomes the whole number part of the mixed number and the second fraction becomes the fraction part of the mixed number. Take a look at the example below:

$\frac{11}{4} = \frac{8+3}{4} = \frac{8}{4} + \frac{3}{4} = 2 + \frac{3}{4}$ OR $2\frac{3}{4}$

TRICK:

This is a very useful way of finding remainders, the 3 in the example above.

---

12. Converting a Fraction to a Decimal

Method 1

Convert to an equivalent fraction whose denominator is a power of 10, such as 10, 100, 1000, 10000, and so on, then write in decimal form by moving the decimal point from the very right to the left a number of times equal to the number of zeros in the denominator.

Examples:

$$\frac{1}{4} = \frac{1 \times 25}{4 \times 25} = \frac{25}{100} = 0.25$$

We multiplied the numerator and denominator by 25 to make the denominator equal to 100
(25 X 4 = 100). Then we moved a decimal point from the right of the "5" two places (because 100 has two zeros) to the left.

Method 2

Divide the numerator by the denominator using regular division.

Example:

$$\frac{13}{4} = 13 \div 4 = 3.25$$

13. Adding and Subtracting Fractions

A. If the fractions have the same denominator:

* Their sum is the sum of the numerators over the denominator.

Example:

$$\frac{3}{8} + \frac{2}{8} = \frac{5}{8}$$

* Their difference is the difference of the numerators over the denominator.

Example:

$$\frac{3}{8} - \frac{2}{8} = \frac{1}{8}$$

Remember: You should never add or subtract the denominators!

B. If the fractions have different denominators:

1) First, find the least common denominator.
2) Then write equivalent fractions using this denominator.
3) Add or subtract the fractions. Reduce if necessary.

Example:

$$\frac{3}{4} - \frac{1}{6} = ?$$

1. The least common denominator (The least common multiple of 4 & 6) is 12.

2. $\frac{9}{12}$ is equivalent to $\frac{3}{4}$ and $\frac{2}{12}$ is equivalent to $\frac{1}{6}$

3. $\frac{3}{4} - \frac{1}{6} = \frac{9}{12} - \frac{2}{12} = \frac{7}{12}$

14. Adding and Subtracting Mixed Numbers

To add or subtract mixed numbers, simply convert the mixed numbers into improper fractions, then add or subtract them as fractions.

Example:

$$9\frac{1}{2} + 5\frac{3}{4} =$$

Converting each number to an improper fraction, we get:

$$9\frac{1}{2} = \frac{19}{2} \quad \& \quad 5\frac{3}{4} = \frac{23}{4}$$

We want to calculate $\frac{19}{2} + \frac{23}{4}$. The LCM of 2 and 4 is 4.

So, $\frac{19}{2} + \frac{23}{4} = \frac{38}{4} + \frac{23}{4} = \frac{61}{4}$

15. Multiplying Fractions and Fractions

When two fractions are multiplied, we multiply both numerators and their result becomes the numerator of the answer. Then we multiply both denominators and their result becomes the denominator of the answer.
Example:

$$\frac{3}{7} \times \frac{5}{2} = \frac{3 \times 5}{7 \times 2} = \frac{15}{14}$$

16. Multiplying Fractions and Whole Numbers

To multiply a fraction by a whole number, write the whole number as an improper fraction with a denominator of 1, then multiply as fractions.

Example:

$3 \times \dfrac{5}{2}$. We can write the number 3 as $\dfrac{3}{1}$. Now we multiply the fractions.

$$\dfrac{3}{1} \times \dfrac{5}{2} = \dfrac{15}{2}$$

---

17. Multiplying Mixed Numbers

To multiply mixed numbers, convert them to improper fractions and multiply.

Example:

$$9\dfrac{1}{2} \times 5\dfrac{3}{4} =$$

Converting to improper fractions, we get

$$9\dfrac{1}{2} = \dfrac{19}{2} \quad \& \quad 5\dfrac{3}{4} = \dfrac{23}{4}$$

So the answer is

$$\dfrac{19}{2} \times \dfrac{23}{4} = \dfrac{19 \times 23}{2 \times 4} = \dfrac{437}{8}$$

18. Dividing Fractions

To divide a fraction by another fraction, multiply the first fraction by the reciprocal of the second fraction. Look at the following examples:

$$\frac{3}{4} \div \frac{5}{7} = \frac{3}{4} \times \frac{7}{5} = \frac{21}{20}$$

$$\frac{2}{3} \div \frac{7}{4} = \frac{2}{3} \times \frac{4}{7} = \frac{8}{21}$$

Notes:

1. If you are dividing a whole number by a fraction or a fraction by a whole number, simply write the whole number as a fraction with a denominator of 1 then solve as explained above. Confused? Well, here's an example:

Example:

$$\frac{2}{3} \div 7 = \frac{2}{3} \div \frac{7}{1} = \frac{2}{3} \times \frac{1}{7} = \frac{2}{21}$$

2. If you are asked to divide mixed numbers, just convert them to improper fractions then proceed like explained above.

Example:

$$9\frac{1}{2} \div 5\frac{3}{4} = ?$$

First convert them into improper fractions, so the question becomes:

$$\frac{19}{2} \div \frac{23}{4} =$$

$$\frac{19}{2} \div \frac{23}{4} = \frac{19}{2} \times \frac{4}{23} = \frac{76}{46}$$

Remember that multiplying or dividing the numerator by the same number gives us an equivalent form of the fraction. So, to make this fraction simpler we can divide the numerator and denominator by 2. This will give us

$$\frac{76}{46} = \frac{76 \div 2}{46 \div 2} = \frac{38}{23}$$

---

19. Simplifying Complex Fractions

A complex fraction is a fraction whose numerator or denominator is also a fraction or mixed number. To solve these types of fractions, simply rewrite the question as a division question.

Example:

$$\frac{\frac{2}{3}}{\frac{7}{5}} = \frac{2}{3} \div \frac{7}{5} = \frac{2}{3} \times \frac{5}{7} = \frac{10}{21}$$

3. Decimals

1. Place Values of Decimal Numbers

2. Expanded Form of a Decimal Number

3. Adding Decimals

4. Subtracting Decimals

5. Comparing Decimal Numbers

6. Rounding Decimal Numbers

7. Estimating Sums and Differences

8. Multiplying Decimal Numbers

9. Dividing Decimals and Whole Numbers

10. Dividing Decimals by Decimals

1. Place Values of Decimal Numbers

The places to the left of the decimal point are ones, tens, hundreds, and so on, just as with whole numbers. The places to the right of the decimal point are called tenths, hundredths, thousandths, and so on. Look at the table below. Please.

Place (underlined)	Name of Position
<u>1</u>.234567	Ones (units) position
1.<u>2</u>34567	Tenths
1.2<u>3</u>4567	Hundredths
1.23<u>4</u>567	Thousandths
1.234<u>5</u>67	Ten thousandths
1.2345<u>6</u>7	Hundred Thousandths
1.23456<u>7</u>	Millionths

Example:

In the number 3.564, the 3 is in the ones place, the 5 is in the tenths place, the 6 is in the hundredths place, and the 4 is in the thousandths place.

Note:

Adding extra zeros to the right of the last decimal digit does not change the value of the decimal number. That means, for example, that 3.12 is the same as 3.120 and 5.15 is the same as 5.150

---

2. Expanded Form of a Decimal Number

The expanded form of a decimal number is the number written as the sum of its whole number and decimal place values.

Example:

3 + 0.7 + 0.01 + 0.002 is the expanded form of the number 3.712.

100 + 5 + 0.06 is the expanded form of the number 105.06.

3. Adding Decimals

To add decimals, line up the decimal points and then follow the rules for adding whole numbers. Make sure to arrange the decimal points properly under each other..

When one number has more decimal places than another, use 0's to give them the same number of decimal places.

Example:

75.69 + 52.37

1) Line up the decimal points:

```
 75.69
+52.37
```

2) Then add.

```
 75.69
+52.37
128.06
```

Example:

12.924 + 3.61

* Add a zero to 3.61 making it 3.610 so it would have three digits to the right of the decimal
   point like 12.924

1) Line up the decimal points:

```
  12.924
+  3.610
```

2) Then add.

```
  12.924
+  3.610
  ──────
  16.534
```

4. Subtracting Decimals

Just as we did in addition, to subtract decimals, line up the decimal points and then follow the rules for subtracting whole numbers. Make sure to arrange the decimal points properly under each other.

When one number has more decimal places than another, use 0's to give them the same number of decimal places.

Example:

18.2 - 6.008

* Add two zeros to 18.2 making it 18.200 so it would have three digits to the right of the decimal
   point like 6.008

1) Line up the decimal points.

18.200

-

 6.008

2) Subtract.

```
  18.200
-  6.008
  ------
  12.192
```

---

5. Comparing Decimal Numbers

Compare the whole numbers to the left of the decimal point.

* **If they are not the same**, the smaller decimal number is the one with the smaller whole number.

Example:

Compare 50.689 with 45.236

50.689   45.236

50 is bigger than 45, so the bigger decimal number is 50.689

We write 50.689 > 45.236   or   45.236 < 50.689

* **If they are the same**, compare the whole number to the right of the decimal point.
  The smaller decimal number is the one with the smaller whole number on the right of the
   decimal point.

Example:

Compare 25.802 with 25.704

25.**802**   25.**704**

The whole numbers to the left of the decimal point are equal, so compare the whole numbers to the right of the decimal point.

704 is smaller than 802, so the smaller decimal number is 25.704

We write 25.704 < 25.802   or   25.802 > 25.704

NOTE:

Sometimes, the numbers may not have the same number of decimal places to the right of the decimal point. In that case we just add extra zeros so that both numbers have the same number of digits after the decimal point.

Example:

Compare 10.528 with 10.61

add a 0 after 10.61 to get 10.610

610 is bigger than **528**, so 10.528 < 10.61

Be careful, if you hadn't added the zero, you would have compared 528 with 61. In that case, the answer would have been wrong.

6. Rounding Decimal Numbers

When we round a number to any decimal place value:

- We want to find a number with zeros in all of the lower places (to the right of the place we are rounding to).
- The number in the place we are rounding to either stays as it (if the number after it is 0,1,2,3, or 4) OR increases by 1 (if the number after it is 5,6,7,8, or 9).

Examples:

Rounding 1.19 to the nearest tenth gives 1.2   (Which is the same as 1.20).

Rounding 1.547 to the nearest hundredth gives 1.55.   (Which is the same as 1.550)

Rounding 1.80 to the nearest one gives 2.   (Which is the same as 2.0)

---

7. Estimating Sums and Differences

We can use rounding to get quick estimates on sums and differences of decimal numbers. First round each number to the place value you choose, then add or subtract the rounded numbers to estimate the sum or difference.

Example:

To estimate the sum 119.25 + 0.67 to the nearest whole number, first round each number to the nearest one, giving us 119 + 1, then add to get 120.

8. Multiplying Decimal Numbers

To multiply decimals:

Simply multiply the numbers as whole numbers (without any decimal points) and write your answer.

The next step is to put the decimal point back in the answer. To do this, add the **number** of digits (not the digits, just the number of digits) to the right of the decimal point in each of the numbers you are multiplying in the original question. The result is how many places to the left, in the final answer, you should put a decimal point at. Don't worry; it's easier once you read the examples.

Example:

4.032×4

We can multiply 4032 by 4 to get 16128

There are **three** decimal places in 4.032 and none in 4, so place the decimal **three** digits to the left:

$4.032 \times 4 = 16.128$ (See where we put the decimal point in 16.128? **Three** digits to the left)

Example:

6.74×9.063

We can multiply 674 by 9063 to get 6108462

There are **5** decimal places: **two** in the number 6.74 and **three** in the number 9.063, so place the decimal point **five** digits to the left:

$6.74 \times 9.063 = 61.08462$

9. Dividing Decimals and Whole Numbers

A. To divide a decimal by a whole number:

Ignore the decimal point and simply divide the two numbers as whole numbers.

Then put a decimal point a number of times to the left equal to the number of digits to the right of the decimal point in the decimal number in the question. Now, that's confusing! Example, please.

Example:

4.9 ÷ 7

First calculate 49 ÷ 7 = 7

Then add the decimal point **one** place to the left of 7 because there was only **one** digit"9" to the right of the original decimal number in the question "4.9"

So the answer is 0.7

Similarly:
5.55 ÷ 5 = 1.11   (We did 555÷5 = 111 the we put the decimal point two places to the left)

B. To divide a whole number by a decimal:

Ignore the decimal point and simply divide the two numbers as whole numbers.

Then put zeros to the right of the answer a number of times equal to the number of digits to the right of the decimal point in the decimal number in the question. Still confusing? Here's an example.

Example:

49 ÷ 0.7

First calculate 49 ÷ 7 = 7

Then add one zero to the right of 7 because there was only **one** digit"7" to the right of the original decimal point in the question "0.7"

So the answer is 70

Similarly:
49 ÷ 0.07 = 700   (Because there were two digits after the decimal point, we added two zeros)

---

10. Dividing Decimals by Decimals

To divide a decimal number by another decimal number, multiply both decimals by a power of 10 (10,100,1000, etc.) great enough to obtain a whole number in at least one of them. Then the problem becomes a problem involving whole numbers which can be solved as explained in the previous page.

Example:

0.144 ÷ 0.12

Multiplying both decimals by 100, we get 14.4 ÷ 12. (We multiplied by 100 to get 12 instead of 0.12)

Which can be solved as explained in the previous page by dividing 144 by 12 and adding a decimal point one place to the left of the answer.

144 ÷ 12 = 12

So the answer is 1.2

NOTE:

We could have made both decimal numbers whole numbers by multiplying both by 1000. In that case, the problem would have been 144 ÷ 120 which would have, of course, given us 1.2

4. Ratio and Proportion

1. What is a Ratio?

2. Comparing Ratios

3. Proportions

4. Rate

1. What is a Ratio?

A ratio is a comparison of two numbers.

Suppose we want to write the ratio of 8 and 12.

We can write this as **8:12** or as a fraction $\frac{8}{12}$, and we say the ratio is *eight to twelve*.

But be careful 8:12 is not the same thing as 12:8

Examples:

Sue has a bag with 3 pens, 4 markers, 7 books, and 1 orange.

1) What is the ratio of books to markers?

$\frac{7}{4}$ OR **7 : 4**

Remember:

Order is very important 7:4 is not the same thing as 4:7. The second ratio means that there are 4 books and 7 markers, which is wrong.

---

2. Comparing Ratios

To compare ratios, write them as fractions. The ratios are equal if they are equal when written as fractions.

Example:

Are the ratios 2 to 4 and 1:2 equal?

The ratios are equal if $\frac{2}{4} = \frac{1}{2}$.
These are equal if their cross products are equal; that is, if 2 X 2 = 1 X 4.
Since both of these products equal 4, the answer is **yes, the ratios are equal**.

3. Proportions

A proportion is an equation with a ratio on each side. It is a statement that two ratios are equal.

$\frac{3}{4} = \frac{6}{8}$ is an example of a proportion.

When one of the four numbers in a proportion is unknown, simply cross multiply to find the unknown number.

Example:

Find **n** if $\frac{1}{2} = \frac{n}{4}$

Using cross multiplication, we see that $2 \times n = 1 \times 4 = 4$, therefore $2 \times n = 4$.
Dividing both sides by 2, we get $n = 4 \div 2$ so $n = 2$.

---

4. Rate

A rate is a ratio that expresses how much time it takes to do something, such as driving a certain distance. To drive 5 miles in one hour is to drive at the rate (or speed) of 5 miles per hour. Problems involving rates usually just need writing two ratios equal to each other and solving for the unknown quantity, in other words solving the proportion.

Example:

John runs 5 miles in 2 hours. At that rate, how far could he run in 4 hours?

Set up the proportion:

$$\frac{5\ miles}{2\ hours} = \frac{?\ miles}{4\ hours}$$

Cross multiply to get **5 X 4 = ? X 2**
So **20 = ? X 2**
Therefore **?= 10 miles**

NOTE:

When comparing rates, always check to see which units are being used. 5 kilometers per hour is not the same thing as 5 meters per hour!

When solving any math or science problem it is very important to write out the units when multiplying, dividing, or converting from one unit to another.

NOTE:

Average Speed

The average speed for a trip is the **total distance traveled divided by the total time of the trip**.

Example:

A boy walks 3 km in 2 hours, then runs 6 km in 1 hour. What is the boy's average speed for the distance he traveled?

The total distance traveled is 3 + 6 = 9 km.

The total time for the trip is 2 + 1 = 3 hours.

The average speed for his trip is 9 ÷ 3 = **3 kilometers per hour**.

5. Percents

1. **What is a Percent?**

2. **Percent as a fraction**

3. **Converting a Fraction into a Percent**

4. **Converting Percents and Decimals**

5. **Percent Increase (Markup)**

6. **Percent Decrease (Discount)**

7. **Calculating The New Value After Markup or Increase in Value**

8. **Calculating The New Value After Discount or Decrease in Value**

9. **Common Percent Problems**

1. What is a Percent?

A percent is a ratio of a number to 100. A percent can be expressed using the percent symbol **%**.

Example:

50 percent or **50%** are both the same, and stand for the ratio **50:100** or $\frac{50}{100}$.

Note that $\frac{50}{100} = \frac{1}{2}$. That's why we say that 50% of something is half of that thing. Look below for more details.

NOTE:

Per Cent means Over A Hundred

---

2. Percent as a fraction

A percent is equivalent to a fraction with denominator 100.

Example:

7% of something $= \frac{7}{100}$ of that thing.

Example:

53% most nearly equals which one of the following: $\frac{1}{2}, \frac{3}{4}$ or $\frac{5}{3}$?

$53\% = \frac{53}{100}$. This is very close to $\frac{50}{100}$ which is $\frac{1}{2}$. So the answer is $\frac{1}{2}$

3. Converting a Fraction into a Percent

To convert a fraction into a percent, multiply or divide the numerator and denominator by a number that will change the denominator into 100. The new numerator becomes the percent.

Example:

$\frac{7}{25}$ is what percent?

We want to convert $\frac{7}{25}$ to a fraction with 100 in the denominator.

So multiply the numerator and the denominator by 4 because 4 X 25 = 100

The fraction becomes: $\frac{7}{25} = \frac{7 \times 4}{25 \times 4} = \frac{28}{100}$ so the answer is **28%**

Example:

$\frac{14}{200}$ is what %?

We want to convert $\frac{14}{200}$ to a fraction with 100 in the denominator.

So divide the numerator and the denominator by 2 because 200 ÷ 2 = 100

The fraction becomes: $\frac{14}{200} = \frac{14 \div 2}{200 \div 2} = \frac{7}{100}$ so the answer is **7%**

4. Converting Percents and Decimals

* To convert from a decimal to a percent:

Just move the decimal point 2 places to the right. Don't forget to put the % sign.

For example, 0.17 = 17%.

Example:

0.0005 = 0.05%

* To convert from a percent to a decimal:

Just move the decimal point 2 places to the left.

Be careful, you can only do this if the percent is written as a whole number or decimal.

Example:

Express 5% in decimal form. Moving the decimal point 2 places to the left (and adding in 0's to the left of the 5 as place holders,) we get 0.05

Example:

Express $2\frac{3}{4}$ % in decimal form.

First we write $2\frac{3}{4}$ in decimal form which is **2.75**

Now convert **2.75 %** into a decimal.

So move the decimal point 2 places to the left to get **0.0275**

So $2\frac{3}{4}$% = **0.0275**

5. Percent Increase (Markup)

If the value of something increases, say from $100 to $150, that means that it increased by $50. This $50 increase is 50% of the original $100. This 50% is called the percent increase.

Example:

A gold ring was worth $130 in 2004, and in 2009 its value became $143. What is the percent increase of its price?

The change is $143 - $130 = $13, an increase in price of $13.

Since $13 is 10% of $130, we say its value increased by 10% from 2004 to 2009.

BE CAREFUL:

We always divide the increase in value ($13) by the ORIGINAL price ($130) to get the percent increase. $13 \div 130 = 0.1$ which is 10%. Never divide by the NEW value.

6. Percent Decrease (Discount)

If the value of something decreases, say from $200 to $100, that means that it decreased by $100. This $100 decrease is 50% of the original $200. This 50% is called the percent deccrease.

BE CAREFUL:

We always divide the decrease in value ($100) by the ORIGINAL price ($200) to get the percent decrease. $100 \div 200 = 0.5$ which is 50%. Never divide by the NEW value.

Example:

A restaurant makes a pie that has 8 spoons of sugar. If the recipe is changed so that the pie has only 6 spoons of sugar. What is the percent decrease in the amount of sugar used in the pie?

The change is 8 - 6 = 2 spoons, a decrease of 2 spoons of sugar.

Since 2 is 25% of 8

Remember that we do this by dividing 2 by the original 8 spoons getting 0.25 which is 25%

That means that the pie now has 25% less sugar, or a 25% decrease in sugar.

BE CAREFUL:

We always divide the decrease in value (2 spoons) by the ORIGINAL (8 spoons) to get the percent decrease. Never divide by the NEW value.

7. Calculating The New Value After Markup or Increase in Value

The new value after a markup or increase in value can be found by using the following rule:

Since:

NEW VALUE = OLD VALUE + INCREASE IN VALUE

Then:

NEW VALUE = OLD VALUE + (PERCENT INCREASE X OLD VALUE)

That is, of course, because ***the percent increase X the old value*** gives us the **increase of value**.

So if, for example, the price of something was $100 and increased by 50 %, then the increase of value would equal 50% X $100 which equals $50.

Therefore **The New Value = The old Value ($100) + Increase in value ($50) = $150**

Example:

John pays $5 to buy a bus ticket every day. Starting tomorrow the price of the ticket will increase by 50%. How much will the ticket cost tomorrow?

New Value = Old Value + (Percent Increase X Old Value)

New Value = $ 5   + (50%   X $ 5   )

New Value = $ 5   + (0.5   X $ 5   )

New Value = $ 5   + ($ 2.5   )

New Value = $ 7.5

8. Calculating The New Value After Discount or Decrease in Value

The new value after a discount or decrease in value can be found by using the following rule:

Since:

NEW VALUE = OLD VALUE − DECREASE IN VALUE

Then:

NEW VALUE = OLD VALUE − (PERCENT DECREASE X OLD VALUE)

That is, of course, because *the percent decrease* X *the old value* gives us the **decrease of value**.

So if, for example, the price of something was $100 and decreased by 50 %, then the decrease of value would equal 50% X $100 which equals $50.

Therefore **The New Value = The old Value ($100) − Decrease in value ($50) = $50**

Example:

A shirt costs $40. It is on sale at 50% off. How much will the shirt cost after the dicount?

New Value = Old Value − (Percent Decrease X Old Value)

New Value = $ 40 − (50% X $ 40)

New Value = $ 40 − (0.5 X $ 40)

New Value = $ 40 − ($ 20)

New Value = $ 20

9. Common Percent Problems

A. Something % of a Number

Use the following two tricks:

1. Percent (%) means **over a hundred**

2. **of** means **times (X)**

Example:

What is 30% of 60 ?

Rewrite the question as $\frac{30}{100}$ x 60

So the answer is 18

B. Finding a number given a certain percent of it

Use the following trick:

Answer = (Number not with % sign x 100) ÷ Number with % sign

Examples:

- **If 50% of a number is 30, then that number is?**

Answer = (30 x 100) ÷ 50 = 3000 ÷ 50 = 60

So the answer is 60

- **20 is 250% of what?**

Answer = (20 x 100) ÷ 250 = 2000 ÷ 250 = 8

So the answer is 8

C. Any other type of percent problem

Use the following trick

Answer = (Number NOT after "of" X 100) ÷ (Number after "of")

Examples:

- **18 is what % of 60?**

Answer = (18 X 100) ÷ 60 = 1800 ÷ 60 = 30

So the answer is 30%

- **What % of 60 is 30?**

Answer = (30 X 100) ÷ 60 = 3000 ÷ 60 = 50

So the answer is 50%

- **What percent of 54 is 37?**

Answer = (37 X 100) ÷ 54 = 3700 ÷ 54 = 68.5

So the answer is 68.5%

Important Note:

All the above examples can be solved by putting:

$\dfrac{}{100}$	instead of	%
X	instead of	**"of"**
=	instead of	**"is"**
N (or any letter)	instead of	**what**

Then find N using simple algebra rules.

Example:

If 50% of a number is 30, then that number is? Rewrite it as:

$\dfrac{50}{100}$ x **N** = 30

0.5 x N = 30   *divide both sides by 0.5 to have only "N"*

N = 30 ÷ 0.5   *on the left hand side.*

N = 60

6. Statistics

1. Average or Arithmetic Mean

2. Median

3. Mode

4. Range

May I say:

This chapter reviews some basic rules and definitions of statistics. You will need them to answer some of the questions on the test. Although there's a whole lot more to statistics, the following four points should be sufficient for the test.

1. Average or Arithmetic Mean

The mean of a list of numbers (also called the average) is found by adding all the terms in the list and dividing that sum by the number of terms in the list.

$$\text{Average} = \frac{\text{Sum of terms in the list}}{\text{Number of terms in the list}}$$

Example:

Find the mean of 2, 6, 12, and 8.

We add all the numbers getting 28, and then we divide that sum by the number of terms in the list, which is 4.

$(2 + 6 + 12 + 8) \div 4 = 7$

So the mean or average of these four numbers is 7.

Example:

Find the mean of 12, 5, 10, 11, 7, and 8 to the nearest hundredth.

$(12 + 5 + 10 + 11 + 7 + 8) \div 6 = 8.8333333\ldots$

which is 8.83 rounded to the nearest hundredth.

2. Median

The median of a list of numbers is the value in the middle when the numbers are ordered from least to greatest.

* If the list has an odd number of numbers, the middle number in this list (after ordering) is the median.

Example:

The ages of John's uncles and aunts are 41, 47, 60, 42, 44, 43, and 47. Find the median of their ages.

First place them in order: 41, 42, 43, 44, 47, 47, 60. The middle number is the 4th number which is 44. So the median is 44.

* If the list has an even number of numbers, the median is the sum of the two middle numbers divided by 2 (that's the average of the two middle numbers). Remember to put them in order first.

Example:

The students in Mr. John's class have the following grades: 4, 30, 5, 3, 4, 11, 16, 14, 17, 3. Find the median of their ages.

First place in order: 3, 3, 4, 4, 5, 11, 14, 16, 17, 30.

Since the number of terms is 10, then the middle numbers are 5 and 11, which are the 5th and 6th terms on the ordered list. The median is the average of these two numbers:

$(5 + 11) \div 2 = 16 \div 2 = 8$

NOTE:

In the example above we had two 3s and two 4s, that didn't change anything when we wrote the numbers in order. We just put them next to each other in order.

3. Mode

The mode of a list of numbers is the number that occurs most often. Sometimes there is no mode.

Example:

Tim's dogs have the following ages: 2, 9, 1, 3, 4, 6, 6, 6, 9, 3. Find the mode of their ages.

6, which appears three times, is the number that appeared the most number of times on the list.

So the mode of their ages is 6.

---

4. Range

The range of a list of numbers is the biggest number minus the smallest number in the list.

Example:

Sam's cats have the following ages: 2, 7, 1, 3, 4, 4, 8, 3. Find the range of their ages.

The range is **8** (biggest number) – **1** (smallest number) = **7**

7. Probability

1. What is an event?

2. Possible Outcomes of an Event

3. Probability of an Outcome

4. Notes on Probability

1. What is an event?

An event is an experiment or collection of experiments.

Examples:

The following are examples of events.

1) Tossing a coin.
2) Rolling a die.
3) Drawing a card from a deck of cards.
4) Drawing 4 cards from a deck of cards.
5) Tossing a coin and rolling a die.

---

2. Possible Outcomes of an Event

Possible outcomes of an event are the results that may occur from any event.

Examples:

The following are possible outcomes of events.

1) A coin toss has two possible outcomes. The outcomes are "heads" and "tails".

2) Rolling a regular six-sided die has six possible outcomes. You could get 1, 2, 3, 4, 5, or 6 dots.

3) Drawing a card from a regular deck of 52 playing cards has 52 possible outcomes.

4) Drawing a red colored card from a regular deck of 52 playing cards has 26 possible outcomes because half of the cards (26) are black and half (26) are red.

3. Probability of an Outcome

The probability of an outcome for a certain event is an indication of how likely a particular outcome is to occur (how probable it is).

The probability is the ratio of the number of ways the outcome may occur to the number of total possible outcomes for the event.

$$\text{Probability} = \frac{\textit{The number of ways the outcome may occur}}{\textit{The total possible outcomes}}$$

In other words:

$$\text{Probability} = \frac{\textit{What we want}}{\textit{All the possibilities}}$$

Probability is usually expressed as a fraction or decimal.

The probability of an event is a number from 0 through 1.

A probability of zero means that the outcome is impossible.
Choosing a green card from a regular deck of cards would have a probability of 0 because there are no green cards.

A probability of one means that the outcome must definitely occur.
Choosing a card of any color from a regular deck of cards would have a probability of 1.

Example:

There are 10 cards in a box numbered as follows: 1, 1, 2, 7, 5, 4, 9, 5, 6, and 6. A single card is randomly chosen from the box. What is the probability of drawing a ball numbered 6?

There are 2 ways to draw a 6, since there are two balls numbered 6. The total possible number of outcomes is 10, since there are 10 balls.

So the probability of drawing a 6 is $\frac{2}{10} = \frac{1}{5}$.

4. Notes on Probability

The probability of two independent events is

The Probability of Event 1 x The Probability of Event 2

Example:

Find the probability of getting a heads from a coin toss AND choosing a green marble from a bag containing 3 green marbles and 5 blue marbles.

First, find the probability of getting the heads.

$$\frac{1 \ (heads)}{2 \ (2 \ possibilities: heads \ and \ tails)} = \frac{1}{2}$$

Second, find the probability of choosing the green marble.

$$\frac{3 \ (green \ marbles)}{8 \ (8 \ possibilities: 3 \ green \ and \ 5 \ blue)} = \frac{3}{8}$$

Now, since you want to find the probability of BOTH things happening, multiply both probabilities

So The answer is $\frac{1}{2} \times \frac{3}{8} = \frac{3}{16}$

8. Sequences

1. What is a Sequence?

2. Arithmetic Sequence

3. Geometric Sequence

4. Patterns

May I say:

Most sequences questions on the test can be answered without using the following rules of arithmetic and geometric sequences. However, using those rules saves a lot of time.

1. What is a Sequence?

A sequence is a list of numbers arranged in a certain way. Sequences on the test are usually one of the following:

    A. Arithmetic Sequences like 5, 10, 15, 20, 25…….

    B. Geometric Sequences like 3, 6, 12, 24, 48, …….

    C. Patterns like 1,3,5,1,3,5,1,3,5……………………

---

2. Arithmetic Sequence

An arithmetic sequence is a sequence or series of numbers where the same number is *added* every time to get the next term.

To find any term (n^{th} term) in an arithmetic sequence, use the following rule:

$$a_n = a_1 + (n-1)d$$

a_n: the nth term

a_1: the 1st term,

n: the number of the term we're looking for

d: the difference between any two consecutive terms

Example:

What is the 50th term of the following sequence:

2,4,6,8,10,……………..

The difference is 2 (4 - 2 or 6 – 4 or 8 – 6 or 10 - 8)

$a_n = a_1 + (n-1)d$

$a_{50} = 2 + (50-1)2$

$\phantom{a_{50}} = 2 + (49)2$

$\phantom{a_{50}} = 100$

3. Geometric Sequence

A geometric sequence is a sequence or series of numbers where the same number is *multiplied* every time to get the next term.

To find any term (n^{th} term) in a geometric sequence, use the following rule:

$$a_n = a_1 \times r^{(n-1)}$$

a_n: the nth term

a_1: the 1st term

n: the number of the term we're looking for

r: the ratio between any two consecutive terms (ex: $4 \div 2$ or $8 \div 4$, etc.)

Example:

What is the 8th term of the following sequence:

2, 4, 8, 16, 32,……….

The ratio is 2 ($4 \div 2$ or $8 \div 4$ or $16 \div 8$ or $32 \div 16$)

$a_n = a_1 \times r^{(n-1)}$

$a_8 = 2 \times 2^{(8-1)}$

$\quad = 2 \times 2^7$

$\quad = 2 \times 128$

$\quad = 256$

4. Patterns

The key to answering questions involving patterns is to figure out the pattern. Once you figure out the pattern, just repeat the pattern as many times as necessary to find the term you are looking for.

Example:

The sequence *a, b, c, a, b, c, a, b, c, a, b*, ... is the sequence of the letters **a, b, c** repeating in this pattern.

What is the 100th place in this sequence?

We notice that the pattern is *a,b,c* repeating itself.

If we write *a,b,c* 33 times then c will be the 99th term (33 x 3 letters). This means that the 100th term will be the one after *c* which is *a*

9. Basic Algebra & Word Problems

1. **Variables**

2. **Expressions**

3. **Equations**

4. **Solution of an Equation**

5. **Simplifying Equations**

6. **Combining Like Terms**

7. **Simplifying with Addition and Subtraction**

8. **Simplifying by Multiplication or Division**

9. **Word Problems as Equations**

May I say:

Algebra is not tested on the exam, but it is a very useful tool in solving word problems, which are plenty on the test. I only focus on the basics of Algebra in this chapter. Most problems can be solved mentally if you find all this Algebra stuff scary!

1. Variables

A variable is a letter such as *x, y, or s* that represents a number. For example, we could say that *g* stands for the number of girls in a class and *b* stands for the number of boys in a class.

---

2. Expressions

An expression contains numbers, variables, or both.

Example:

The following are examples of expressions:

5   (just a number)

x   (just a variable)

3 + 7   (a variable and a number)

2 *b* + 5g   (variables and numbers)

Example:

Jon has $100, and Mark has *d* dollars. Write an expression for the total amount of money with both of them.

The total money with them is **100 + *d***.

3. Equations

An equation is a statement in which expressions on one side are equal to expressions on the other side. There must be an equal sign in an equation, no wonder they called it "equation". Many word problems can easily be written down as equations.

Example:

The following are examples of equations:

15 = 2 + 13

x = 7

w + 5 = 12 - *w*

Example:

Translate the following word problem into an equation:

My age in years *y* plus 15 is equal to three times my age, minus 8.

$y + 15 = (3 \times y) - 8$

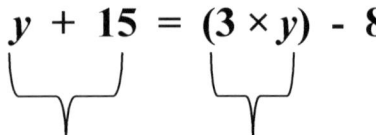

age *y* plus 15   three times my age

4. Solution of an Equation

When an equation has a variable in it, the solution to the equation is the number that makes the equation true when we replace the variable with its value.

Example:

We say **$y = 5$** is a solution to the equation **$3 \times y + 5 = 20$** because replacing *y* with **5** gives us

$3 \times 5 + 5 = 20$

$15 + 5 = 20$

$20 = 20$ which is true.

5. Simplifying Equations

To find a solution to an equation, you need to know some important tricks of simplifying equations. I will discuss each in more detail in the following pages. They are:

1) Combining like terms.

This means adding or subtracting variables of the same kind just as you would do with numbers.

The expression **5X + 2X** should become **7X** because 5 + 2 = 7 and they are both X's.

2) Adding the same value to both sides of the equation.

5 = 6 - 1 is the same as 5 + 2 = 6 - 1 + 2
X = 7 is the same as X + 3 = 7 + 3

3) Subtracting the same value from both sides of the equation.

5 = 5 is the same as 5 - 2 = 5 - 2
X = 7 is the same as X - 3 = 7 – 3

4) Multiplying the same value by both sides of the equation.

4 = 4 is the same as 4 x 2 = 4 x 2
X = 7 is the same as X x 3 = 7 x 3

5) Dividing by the same value in both sides of the equation.

10 = 10 is the same as 10 ÷ 2 = 10 ÷ 2
X = 21 is the same as X ÷ 3 = 21 ÷ 3

6. Combining Like Terms

We use this trick if we have variables (letters) that are the same and are being added or subtracted.

Example:

The number of girls in our school is 50 and that is equal to two times the number of boys plus three times the number of boys in Emma's class. How many boys are in Emma's class?

50 = 2 times the number of boys + 3 times the number of boys

$50 = 2b + 3b$

$50 = 5b$ (Aha! Now combining like terms came in handy: $2b + 3b = 5b$)

So b, the number of boys, equals 10 because 5 x 10 = 50

7. Simplifying with Addition and Subtraction

We can use addition and subtraction to get the variables on one side of the equation without any numbers on that side, and get the numbers on the other side.

Remember whatever you add or subtract on one side, you must also add or subtract on the other side.

Example:

The number of girls in Evan's class plus 5 equals 20. How many girls are in Evan's class?

g + 5 = 20

Now we want to get rid of the 5 so that we only have **g** on the left hand side.
So subtract 5 from both sides.

g + 5 - 5 = 20 – 5

g = 15

8. Simplifying by Multiplication or Division

We can use multiplication and division to get the variables on one side of the equation without any numbers on that side, and get the numbers on the other side.

Remember whatever you multiply or divide on one side, you must also multiply or divide on the other side.

Example:

Find **X** if

$$\frac{X}{4} = 2$$

We want to have just X on the left hand side.
Since X is divided by 4 (over 4), we can multiply both sides by 4 to get just X on the left.

$$\frac{X}{4} \times 4 = 2 \times 4$$

$$X = 8$$

9. Word Problems as Equations

Word problems can be written as equations. Certain words tell you what kind of operations to use: addition, multiplication, subtraction, or division. Here are some common words.

Word	Operation	Example	As an equation
sum	addition	The sum of my age and 5 equals 18.	$y + 5 = 18$
total	addition	The total of my allowance and 20 dollars is $100.	$a + 20 = 100$
more than	addition	Ten more than my age equals 25.	$10 + y = 25$
difference	subtraction	The difference between my age and my brother's age, which is 10 years, is 5 years.	$y - 10 = 5$
less than	subtraction	Four less than Jim's age equals 26.	$y - 4 = 26$
times	multiplication	Three times my age is 45.	$3 \times y = 45$
product	multiplication	The product of my age and 5 is 60.	$y \times 5 = 60$
percent	division by 100	50 percent.	$50 \div 100 = 0.5$
of	usually means times	50 percent of 60.	$50\% \times 60$ $0.5 \times 60 = 30$
is	usually means equals	X is three times 12.	$X = 3 \times 12$

10. Geometry

1. Names of Angles

2. Polygons

3. Types of Triangles and Their Angles

4. Quadrilaterals and Their Angles

5. Area

6. Area of a Square

7. Area of a Rectangle

8. Area of a Triangle

9. Area of a Circle

10. Perimeter

11. Circumference of a Circle

May I say:

Geometry is huge, but fortunately for you (less studying) and for me (less typing), Geometry questions on the test are very limited. You just need the basic definitions and rules in this chapter to be comfortable on the test.

1. Names of Angles

A. Acute Angles

An acute angle is an angle measuring between 0 and 90 degrees.

B. Obtuse Angles

An obtuse angle is an angle measuring between 90 and 180 degrees.

C. Right Angles

A right angle is an angle measuring 90 degrees. Two lines or line segments that meet at a right angle are said to be perpendicular.

Example:

The following angle is a right angle.

90°

D. Complementary Angles

Two angles are called complementary angles if the sum of their degree measurements equals 90 degrees. One of the complementary angles is said to be the complement of the other.

Example:

These two angles are complementary because $50° + 40° = 90°$.

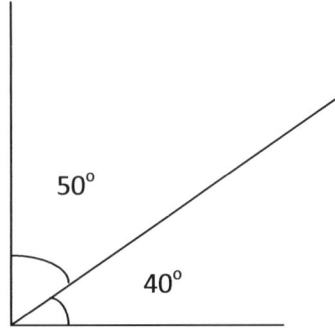

E. Supplementary Angles

Two angles are called supplementary angles if the sum of their degree measurements equals 180 degrees. One of the supplementary angles is said to be the supplement of the other.

Example:

These two angles are supplementary because $120° + 60° = 180°$.

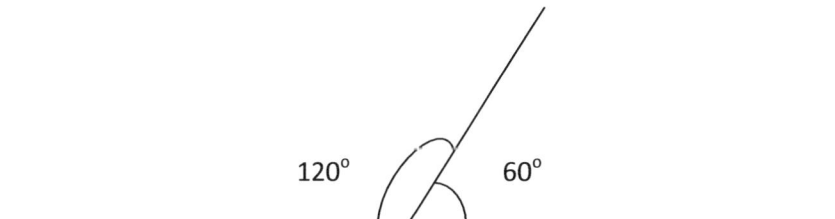

2. Polygons

A polygon is a closed figure made by joining line segments.

The sum of the angles of a polygon with *n* sides is **180° × (*n* - 2)** degrees.

Examples:

The following are examples of polygons:

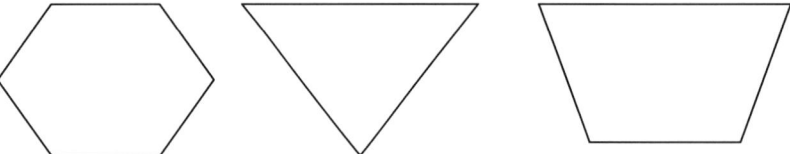

The figure below is not a polygon, since it is not a closed figure:

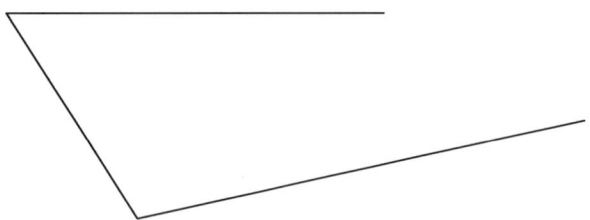

The figure below is not a polygon, since it is not made entirely of line segments:

Note:

Regular Polygons

A regular polygon is a polygon whose sides have equal lengths, and whose angles have equal measures.

Examples:

The following is a regular polygon:

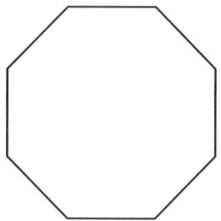

The following is not a regular polygon:

3. Types of Triangles and Their Angles

A. Equilateral Triangle

A triangle having all three sides of equal length. The angles of an equilateral triangle all measure 60 degrees.

Example:

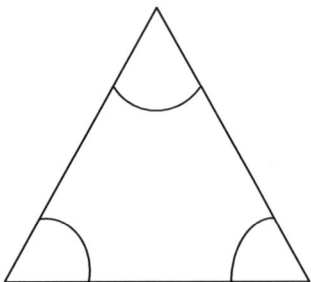

B. Isosceles Triangle

A triangle having two sides of equal length.

The angles opposite to the equal sides are equal.

Example:

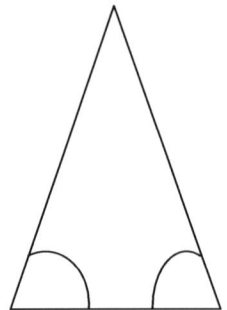

C. Scalene Triangle

A triangle having three sides of different lengths.

Example:

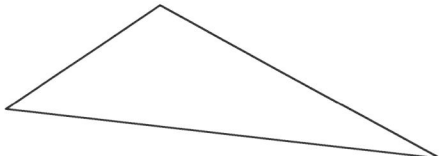

NOTE:

The sum of the angles of a triangle is 180 degrees.

Since it has 3 sides, the sum of angles = 180° x (n-2) = 180° x (3-2) =180°

4. Quadrilaterals and Their Angles

A quadrilateral is a four-sided polygon like a square, rectangle, and rhombus.

The sum of the angles of a quadrilateral is 360 degrees.

Since it has 4 sides, the sum of angles = 180° x (4-2) = 180° x (2) =360°

5. Area

The area of a figure measures the size of the region enclosed by that figure. The unit of area is always a square unit like square meters, square centimeters, or square inches.

6. Area of a Square

If S is the side-length of a square, the area of the square is S^2 or $S \times S$.

Example:

What is the area of a square having sides of length 4 cm each?

The area is $S \times S$. So the area is **4 x 4 = 16 cm^2**

---

7. Area of a Rectangle

The area of a rectangle is the product of its length and width.

Area = L x W

Example:

What is the area of a rectangle having a length of 6 inches and a width of 2 inches?

Area = L x W. So the area = **6 x 2 = 12 in^2**

8. Area of a Triangle

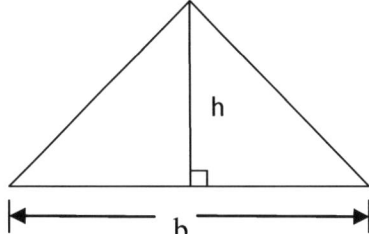

The area of the triangle is $\frac{1}{2} \times$ ***base*** $\times$ ***height***.

Area $= \frac{1}{2} \times b \times h$

The base is any side of the triangle.

The height is the perpendicular line drawn from the opposite vertex (corner) to that base.

Example:

What is the area of a triangle having a base of length 5 cm and a height of 4 cm?

Area $= \frac{1}{2} \times b \times h = \frac{1}{2} \times 5 \times 6 = \frac{1}{2} \times 30 = 15$ cm^2.

9. Area of a Circle

The area of a circle is **Pi × r^2** or **Pi × r × r**, where *r* is the length of its radius.

Pi (π) is a number that is approximately 3.14

$$A = \pi r^2$$

Example:

What is the area of a circle having a radius of 4 cm, to the nearest tenth of a square cm?

$A = \pi r^2 = 3.14 \times 4^2 = 3.14 \times 16 = $ **50.24 cm^2** which is **50.2 cm^2** rounded to the nearest tenth.

---

10. Perimeter

The perimeter of a polygon is the sum of the lengths of all its sides.

Example:

What is the perimeter of a rectangle having side-lengths of 3cm and 8 cm?

Since a rectangle has 4 sides, and the opposite sides of a rectangle have the same length, this rectangle has 2 sides of length 3 cm, and 2 sides of length 8 cm.

The perimeter is 3 + 3 + 8 + 8 = 22 cm.

Example:

What is the perimeter of a square having side-length 12 cm?

Since a square has 4 sides of equal length, the perimeter of the square is **4 x side length**

Perimeter = 4 x 12 = 48 cm or 12 + 12 + 12 + 12 = 48 cm.

Example:

What is the perimeter of a regular *(Remember: "Regular" means all sides are equal)* hexagon, which is a six sided polygon, having side-length 2 m?

A hexagon is a figure having 6 sides, and since this is a regular hexagon, each side has the same length

The perimeter of the hexagon is 6 × 2 = 12 m or 2 + 2 + 2 + 2 + 2 + 2 = 12 m

11. Circumference of a Circle

The circumference is the total length of a circle or, in other words, its perimeter. If a circle were made out of a piece of thread, the perimeter would be the length of that piece of thread when it is straight. **The circumference equals 2 x Pi x the radius.**

Circumference = $2\pi r$

Example:

What is the circumference of a circle with a diameter of 7 cm if $\pi = 3.14$?

Circumference = $2\pi r$ = 2 x 3.14 x 7 = 43.96 cm

11. See You Later Calculator

1. **Calculating The Square Root of a Big Number Ending in Zeros**

2. **Calculating The Square Root of Numbers Multiplied by Each Other**

3. **Calculating The Product of a Range of Integers Including Zero**

4. **Calculating The Sum of All Integers from $-X$ to $+X$**

5. **Know Your numbers**

May I say:

You are not allowed to use a calculator on this test. Most test takers find this frightening, and you probably feel that way too. In this chapter, I'll show you a few tricks that you can use to answer questions that you would normally use a calculator to answer.

1. Calculating The Square Root of a Big Number Ending in Zeros

The square root of any number with 2 zeros at the end of the number is the square root of the part without the zeros with just one zero next to it. I know what you're thinking: calculator, please!

Example:

$\sqrt{3600} = \sqrt{36}$ and a zero = 6 and a zero = 60

Similarly, the square root of a number with 4 zeros at the end of the number is the square root of the part without the zeros with just two zeros next to it.

Example:

$\sqrt{160000} = \sqrt{16}$ and 2 zeros = 4 and 2 zeros = 400

---

2. Calculating The Square Root of Numbers Multiplied by Each Other

To find the square root of numbers multiplied by each other, write each of these numbers as a product of two numbers. Do that in a way that will let you have pairs of the same numbers only. In the example below, I wrote **10 as 2 x 5, 20 as 5 x 4**, and **8 as 2 x 4**. This way I have a pair of 5's, a pair of 2's, and a pair of 4's.

After that simply write the answer as one of each number (from each pair) times the other. That is 2 x 5 x 4 in the example below.

$\sqrt{10 \times 20 \times 8} = \sqrt{2 \times 5 \ \times 5 \times 4 \ \times 2 \times 4} = \sqrt{2 \times 2 \ \times 5 \times 5 \ \times 4 \times 4} = 2 \times 5 \times 4 = 40$

3. Calculating The Product of a Range of Integers Including Zero

The product of any number of integers, positive or negative, will always equal zero if zero is one of the integers involved.

Example:

What is the product of all integers from – 5 to 6?

The answer is zero because multiplying all the integers from -5 to 6 includes multiplying by zero, and any number multiplied by zero equals zero.

---

4. Calculating The Sum of All Integers from – X to + X

The sum of all the integers from a negative integer to the positive of that integer equals zero.

Example:

What is the sum of all integers from – 3 to 3?

The sum is zero because -3 + (-2) + (-1) + 0 +1 +2 +3 = 0 since each positive integer will cancel out with its negative friend (friend..huh!) leaving just poor old zero.

5. Know Your Numbers

Make sure you know these famous percents, decimals, and fractions. This will save you precious time on the test.

Percent	Decimal	Fraction
1%	0.01	$1/100$
5%	0.05	$1/20$
10%	0.1	$1/10$
12½%	0.125	$1/8$
20%	0.2	$1/5$
25%	0.25	$1/4$
33⅓%	0.333…	$1/3$
50%	0.5	$1/2$
75%	0.75	$3/4$
80%	0.8	$4/5$
90%	0.9	$9/10$
99%	0.99	$99/100$
100%	1	1
125%	1.25	$5/4$
150%	1.5	$3/2$

12. The Essay

A. Facts About The BCA Essay

B. The Format of The Essay

C. Important Writing Techniques
1. Transitions
2. Choice of Words

D. Important Tricks
1. Beware of Pronoun Agreement
2. Don't Write an Ambiguous Pronoun
3. Don't Use The Passive Voice
4. Avoid Using *ing* with *the*, *pronouns*, and *apostrophes*
5. Don't Confuse These Words

E. Sample Essays

May I say:
Use the following rules and tricks to write a high scoring essay. Also, feel free to send me an essay you write by email or at www.kareemgouda.com , and I'll be glad to mark it and send you my comments.

A. Facts About The BCA Essay

The essay is an important part of your test. Writing an excellent essay will not only bring you closer to being accepted but it will also give you much needed confidence for the rest of the exam and admission process.

You will be given **forty minutes** to read an article and write an essay response. This article is usually a one or two page story. Remember to practice finishing your essay at home in 30 minutes because 40 minutes on the test are not like 40 minutes at home.

The essay is scored using the following criteria:

1. Comprehension (your understanding of the story)
2. Insight (your clear thesis or opinion)
3. Organization (a properly structured 5 paragraph essay)
4. Support (parts of the article that prove your opinion)
5. Style (a clear high school level voice)
6. Grammar and spelling (add to that legible handwriting)

The following pages will address each of the above criteria. More practice and explanation are available through our online classes.

B. The Format of The Essay

The essay should be written using the famous five paragraph format. It is also acceptable to write a four paragraph essay; however, the five paragraph essay is more popular, fills up more space, and is more impressive. The five paragraph essay is more difficult and more time consuming, but remember that you are up against significant competition so all you need to do is practice and then practice some more.

The Five Paragraph Essay:

PARAGRAPH 1: The Introduction

PARAGRAPH 2: Body Paragraph 1

PARAGRAPH 3: Body Paragraph 2

PARAGRAPH 4: Body Paragraph 3

PARAGRAPH 5: The Conclusion

Details will follow.

PARAGRAPH 1: The Introduction

The first paragraph should have at least one clear sentence that states your opinion or what you're going to say in your essay; this sentence is also known as the thesis sentence. It is always best to have a short, clear thesis sentence. In other words, make sure the essay reader can see a clear answer (opinion) to the question. The thesis sentence is the most important part of your essay. Before your thesis sentence, you should write a scene setting sentence which is basically a fancy way of saying that you should write an introduction to your opinion such as a quote or anecdote that serves as an introduction to your thesis sentence. Finally, you should write a hint sentence which basically tells the reader the main points you will discuss in each of the following body paragraphs (paragraphs 2, 3, and 4). The whole introduction should make your main idea clear to the reader. To summarize, your introduction should look like this:

1. Scene Setting Sentence
2. Thesis (opinion) Sentence
3. Hints on the main points presented in the body.

Example*:

   [Scene Setting Sentence] Franklin D. Roosevelt, both a polio victim and the 32nd president of the United States, once stated, "Persistence in face of hardship is the hallmark of individuals who have shaped the world." *[Thesis Sentence]* Adversity can only be overcome by persistence. *[Hints on Your Examples]* George's insistence to buy the jacket and his long visit to his uncle show how hardship can be overturned. Furthermore, George's speech during the dinner party proves that persistence is the only way to overcome adversity.

* This example and the ones on the following pages are written just to show you how each paragraph should look like. They are not related to a particular story or question.

PARAGRAPH 2: Body Paragraph 1

* You should start this paragraph with a topic sentence that shows what specific topic you will discuss in this paragraph. This sentence serves as a transition from the previous paragraph.

* Use specific support, or proof, as evidence of your opinion. Here you should write relevant details that support your topic. The word "relevant" here is very important. Irrelevant details will almost always confuse your reader and create a negative impression. If your essay is about a passage or story (it usually is), you should use proof from the passage or story.

* Always remind the reader, briefly, that the proof you are using is pretty good. This is called a closing sentence. To summarize, your body paragraph should look like this:

    1. Topic Sentence. A transition from the previous paragraph and an introduction to this example paragraph.
    2. Relevant Details. Specific proof that you get from the passage.
    3. Closing Sentence. A sentence that relates the example you just wrote to the thesis (opinion) of your essay.

Example:
    [Topic Sentence]An instance that clearly shows how persistence can lead to success is when George bought the jacket. ***[Relevant Details]***George did not settle for Mr. Maikan's decision; instead, he fought to get what he wanted. George clearly stated his willingness to stay all day at the shop when he said, "this is my jacket; I saw it first, and I'm willing to stay here on the floor blocking this door all day and all night if I have to." Consequently, Mr. Maikan had no other choice than to pay the other customer back and sell the mysterious jacket to George. ***[Closing Sentence]***George's resilience clearly shows that by not giving up he was able to succeed and save his neighbor from a catastrophe.

PARAGRAPHS 3 and 4 *(the other two body paragraphs) should be written the same way. Be sure to add transitions though (we'll talk about transitions in just a little).*

PARAGRAPH 5: The Conclusion

In the conclusion, you should reword your thesis sentence (remember, from the introduction) and briefly summarize the three proofs you used in paragraphs 2 to 4. Also, adding a closing sentence such as a quote or anecdote can be a nice touch. To summarize, your conclusion should look like this:

1. Summary of the 3 Proofs (Topics) from Paragraphs 2, 3 & 4.
2. Thesis (opinion) Sentence.
3. Closing Sentence.

Example:

*[**Summary of Your Examples**]* George's resilience at the shop, his adventure during his visit to his uncle, and his eloquent talk at the party clearly show the relationship between resilience and success. *[**Thesis Sentence**]*Clearly, persistence is the road to success. *[**Closing Sentence**]*My grandfather, a champion boxer was fond of saying, "endure the pain….. appreciate the gain."

C. Important Writing Techniques

1. Transitions:

Transitions are very important words that glue pieces of your essay together. There are many transitions such as **however, nevertheless, furthermore, moreover, consequently, as a result, ultimately,** and **finally**. These transitions should be used at the beginnings of paragraphs or within sentences to explain the relationship between ideas. Following are some examples of some popular relationships and transition words that represent these relationships.

Addition:
also, again, as well as, besides, coupled with, furthermore, in addition, likewise, moreover, similarly.

Consequence:
accordingly, as a result, consequently, for this reason, for this purpose, hence, otherwise, so then, subsequently, therefore, thus.

Contrast and Comparison:
contrast, by the same token, conversely, instead, likewise, on the one hand, on the other hand, on the contrary, rather, similarly, yet, but, however, still, nevertheless, in contrast.

Emphasis
above all, chiefly, especially, particularly, singularly

Exception:
aside from, barring, beside, except, excepting, excluding, exclusive of, other than, outside of.

Exemplifying:

chiefly, especially, for instance, in particular, markedly, namely, particularly, including, specifically, such as.

Generalizing:

as a rule, as usual, for the most part, generally, generally speaking, ordinarily, usually

Illustration:

for example, for instance, for one thing, as an illustration, illustrated with, as an example, in this case.

Similarity:

comparatively, coupled with, correspondingly, identically, likewise, similar, moreover.

Restatement:

in essence, in other words, namely, that is, that is to say, in short, in brief, to put it differently.

Sequence:

at first, first of all, to begin with, in the first place, at the same time, for now, for the time being, the next step, in time, in turn, later on, meanwhile, next, then, soon, the meantime, later, while, earlier, simultaneously, afterward, in conclusion, with this in mind.

Summarizing:

after all, all in all, all things considered, briefly, by and large, in brief, in conclusion, on the whole, in short, in summary, in the final analysis, in the long run, to sum up, to summarize, finally.

2. Choice of words:

In the following pages I will give you examples of better words to use instead of other, easier words, in your essay. I will leave the right part of the page blank so that you can write your own notes and choose the words that you will memorize to use on test day.

A. When writing action verbs use the following verbs:

began

commenced
incited
initiated
introduced
launched
originated
pioneered
instigated
instituted

agreed

acknowledged
assented
conceded
concurred
consented

arrived

appeared
disembarked
alighted
entered
reached

attacked

besieged
pounced
rushed
stormed
assaulted
bombarded
charged
invaded
jumped

closed

blocked
bolted
clenched
clogged
corked
locked
obstructed
sealed

broke

severed
tore
shattered
cracked
crushed
demolished
fractured

chased

hounded
pursued
tracked
drove
followed
trailed

bumped

thudded
thumped
banged
butted
collided
jarred
jolted
jostled
knocked
pounded
rattled
slammed
smacked

changed

adapted
transformed
transposed
altered
mutated
evolved
metamorphosed
revolutionized

cheered

applauded
hailed
praised
saluted

fought

battled
brawled
clashed
disputed
dueled
grappled
jousted
quarreled
skirmished
wrestled

gathered

corralled
herded
hoarded
huddled
aggregated
collected
congregated
convened
converged
rallied

found

discovered
pinpointed
recovered
spotted
uncovered
unearthed

gave

awarded
bequeathed
conferred
contributed
endowed
entrusted
gifted
granted
presented
provided

answered

reacted
remarked
replied
responded
retorted
returned

argued

bickered
contended
contested
contradicted
countered
debated
denied
disagreed
disputed

explained

clarified
described
detailed
illustrated
interpreted
paraphrased
summarized

B. Use the following adverbs when describing actions:

easily

effortlessly
simply
skillfully
smoothly

carefully

attentively
cautiously
mindfully
prudently
vigilantly
watchfully

happily

cheerfully
contentedly
ecstatically
joyfully
merrily

angrily

bitterly
coldly
furiously
indignantly
sharply

beautifully

alluringly
charmingly
elegantly
enchantingly
glamorously
majestically

calmly

harmoniously
peacefully
placidly
serenely
soothingly
tranquilly

hesitantly

falteringly
haltingly
indecisively
irresolutely
reluctantly
tentatively
uncertainly

purposely

consciously
deliberately
intentionally
voluntarily
willfully

quickly

briskly
busily
hastily
hurriedly
impatiently
speedily
swiftly

sadly

despondently
sorrowfully
dismally
cheerlessly
dejectedly
dolefully

strangely

oddly
miraculously
mysteriously

wisely

prudently
discerningly
judiciously
sagaciously

C. Use these words when describing characters:

brave

audacious
gallant
valiant
bold
chivalrous
courageous
dauntless
valorous

cowardly

timid
weak
gutless
spineless

bossy

controlling
demanding
domineering
overbearing
tyrannical

D. Important Tricks

1. Beware of Pronoun Agreement

A singular noun must have a singular pronoun referring to it.
A plural noun must have a plural pronoun referring to it.

Note:

Use **they** to refer to **people** (or any other plural noun)
Use **he or she** to refer to **a person** (or any singular noun that could mean boy or girl)

I personally prefer sticking to **people** in your essay if you are referring to people in general..

2. Don't Write an Ambiguous Pronoun

It must be perfectly clear who or what a pronoun refers to.

John told Patrick that *he* won the competition. *Who won? John? Patrick?*
After tomorrow's test, *they* will announce the winners. *Who will announce?*

3. Don't Use The Passive Voice

I read the book is almost always better than **The book was read by me**.

4. Avoid Using *ing* with *the*, *pronouns*, and *apostrophes*

The + ing.

Don't write: **The** reschedul**ing** of the competition made me sad.

Pronoun + ing.

Don't write: **His** winn**ing** made his parents proud.

's + ing.

Don't write: John**'s** winn**ing** made his parents proud.

These forms are all considered wordy forms and should not be used in your essay.

5. Don't Confuse These Words

1. It's and Its

It's means "**it is**"
Its means belongs to **it**

2. You're and Your

You're means "**you are**"
Your means belongs to **you**

3. They're and Their

They're means "**they are**"
Their means belongs to **them**

4. Principal and Principle

A **Principal** is usually a person who leads a school
A **principle** is a basic truth

5. Except and Accept

Except means left out, like an exception to a rule
Accept means receiving something

6. Effect and Affect

Effect is a noun
Affect is a verb that means to make an effect

7. Advice and Advise

Advice is a noun
Advise is a verb that means to give advice

You can find many more confusable words like those. Email me for a list or search the internet. A good source is *http://oxforddictionaries.com/words/commonly-confused-words*.

E. Sample Essays

Now take a look at the following pages. You'll find sample essays answering the question:

Why do you believe Mrs. Price acted the way she did?

The short story you are being asked about is called <u>Eleven</u> by Sandra Cisneros. At the time of publication, this story is available on the Bergen Academies website. If for any reason you can't find it just email me for a copy. I can't include the story here in this book because I respect its copyrights.

Essay 1:

    Mrs. Price had multiple reasons for her actions. Firstly, she wanted to rid the sweater from her coatroom, and secondly, the whole situation was slowing down her class. Had Mrs. Price handled everything in a calmer, more understanding manner, things might have been resolved without so much of a problem. A simple move could have turned everything around for the better.

    The sweater had been in the coatroom for over a month. Mrs. Price wanted the owner to claim it so that she wouldn't have to deal with it anymore. She was willing to do whatever was necessary, even if that meant wrongfully accusing a student. She apparently didn't care who ended up with the sweater, because she gave it to Rachel when Sylvia Saldivar suggested that it was Rachel's. Then after that, Phyllis Lopez received it after claiming it.

    "Mrs. Price is already turning to page thirty – two, math problem number four." Before Rachel is able to gather herself, Mrs. Price has started to resume her mathematics lesson. Mrs. Price seemed to have no regard for Rachel's discomfort, but rather for the continuation of the math lesson. She wanted to keep the class moving, and did so by abruptly ending the altercation with Rachel.

    Ultimately, Mrs. Price didn't handle the situation in a reasonable way, and because of that, it ended in tears. Rachel was overtly upset because it happened on her birthday, and she was completely innocent. With a considerate attitude, Mrs. Price could have turned everything around for the better.

My Comments on Essay 1:

The Good:

- The writer divided the essay into paragraphs with a clear introduction and conclusion.
- The writer clearly stated the two reasons that made Mrs. Price act this way in the introduction.
- The writer quoted the passage in paragraph 3 to show her evidence.
- The writer used a transition in the final paragraph, "ultimately".

The Bad:

- The writer only used 4 paragraphs instead of 5
- The distinction between the thesis sentence and the hints sentence was not clear in the introduction.
- There was no scene setting sentence in the introduction.
- The conclusion lacks a summary of the points discussed in the body paragraphs.

Essay 2:

In the story "Eleven", the author, Sandra Cisneros, writes about a girl named Rachel and what she went through on her eleventh birthday. Rachel's teacher, Mrs. Price, found a red sweater and asked the class if it belonged to anybody. A girl named Sylvia said that the sweater belonged to Rachel. Thus, Mrs. Price put it on Rachel's desk without even asking whether it belonged to Rachel or not. She even made Rachel put it on!

I believe that Mrs. Price acted the way she did because she wanted to get rid of the sweater. Although it was not necessary to make Rachel wear the sweater, Mrs. Price was just doing her job and returning the sweater to its owner. Sadly, Rachel was not the owner. She tried telling Mrs. Price that it was not hers. In her defense, she had said '"That's not, I don't, you're not...not mine."' Instead of freeing herself of the sweater, Rachel ended up being humiliated in front of her whole class. Phyllis, another student realized that the sweater belonged to her. Rachel gave the sweater to its rightful owner, nevertheless Mrs. Price pretended like everything was okay.

Furthermore, Mrs. Price made another mistake when she forced Rachel to wear the sweater even though Rachel insisted that the sweater was not hers. '"Rachel," Mrs. Price [had said], "you put that sweater on right now and no more nonsense."' Rachel tries to tell Mrs. Price once again that the sweater was not hers but Mrs. Price yells "Now!" and so Rachel puts it on not wanting to get in trouble. This shows that Mrs. Price did make a mistake by forcing Rachel to wear a sweater that was not hers yet, she did not apologize to Rachel after being proven wrong.

In conclusion, Mrs. Price behaved the way she did because she was aggravated that "[the sweater] has been in the coatroom for a month." Also, she was just doing her job and trying to be a kind person by returning the sweater, although I disagree with her ways. Along with Mrs. Price, Rachel was also at fault. She should have been brave and should have stood up for herself.

If I were in Rachel's position, I would have told Mrs. Price that the sweater was not mine from the beginning, or, I would have held on to the sweater until I found its rightful owner. However, I would still expect Mrs. Price to apologize for her harsh actions. She could have been nicer while trying to return the sweater; after all, it was Rachel's eleventh birthday.

My Comments on Essay 2:

The Good:

- The writer divided the essay into 5 paragraphs.
- The writer clearly stated the reasons that made Mrs. Price act this way (although not in the introduction).
- The writer quoted the passage in paragraphs 2, 3 & 4 to show her evidence.
- The writer used transitions well in all paragraphs (can you find them?).

The Bad:

- The 5 paragraphs were not organized properly. Paragraphs 1 & 2 should have been merged into one paragraph (the introduction).
- The reasons for Mrs. Price's actions are not clear in the introduction.
- The last 2 paragraphs should have been merged into one paragraph (the conclusion).
- Overall, this essay, although divided into 5 paragraphs, can be rewritten into only 3 paragraphs. The whole point of the 5 paragraph essay is to develop three topics (or reasons or examples) to prove your thesis (opinion).
- The conclusion lacks a summary of the points discussed in the body paragraphs.

Essay 3:

"Today I wish I was one hundred and two instead of eleven because if I was one hundred and two I'd have known what to say when Mrs. Price put the red sweater on my desk," stated Rachel who celebrated her eleventh birthday but wished she was one hundred and two because of Mrs. Price's actions. Rachel's teacher, Mrs. Price insisted that the sweater belonged to Rachel to prove that she is in control of her classroom. This notion clearly develops through three stages; first, Mrs. Price wants to prove that she controls her class, then she wants to avoid ruining her lesson. Finally, Mrs. Price continues her actions to avoid embarrassing herself.

Mrs. Price, like most teachers, wanted to prove her dominance over her classroom. She achieves this feat by ending the mystery of the red sweater that has been sitting there for a month; "It's been sitting in the coatroom for a month," Mrs. Price said. After the whole class denies she insists, "It has to belong to somebody." At this point, Mrs. Price feels that she will lose control over her classroom. Hence, she is desperate for someone to claim the sweater so that she can move on. Immediately, Sylvia Saldivar says, "I think it belongs to Rachel." Sylvia's words were the solution for Mrs. Price.

As a result of Sylvia's words, Mrs. Price hurried to give Rachel the sweater. Even though Rachel denied that the sweater was hers, Mrs. Price simply stated, "Of course it's yours. I remember you wearing it once." Mrs. Price was obviously trying to avoid ruining her lesson and thus chose Rachel to become her scapegoat. Rachel summarized Mrs. Prices's actions when she said, "because she's older and the teacher, she's right and I'm not." Clearly Mrs. Price did not want any more time waste. Consequently she moves on with her lesson as Rachel describes, "Not mine, not mine, not mine, but Mrs. Price is already turning to page thirty-two, and math problem number four." Mrs. Price has finally gotten rid of the sweater.

The final reason for Mrs. Price's actions is that she wants to avoid being embarrassed in front of her class. When Physllis, the real owner of the sweater reveals herself, Mrs. Price ignores the news and does not even apologize to Rachel. Rachel recounts this incident by saying, "That stupid Phyllis Lopez, who is even dumber than Sylvia Saldivar, says she remembers the red sweater is hers! I take it off right away and give it to her, only Mrs. Price pretends like everything's okay." Because this incident happened towards the end of the lesson, it is clear that Mrs. Price was no longer weary of losing control over her classroom but was, in fact, avoiding the embarrassment of making a completely wrong decision and sticking to it.

In conclusion, Mrs. Price behaved the way she did because she was at first determined to show her dominance over the classroom. Moreover, she insisted on her actions to save herself from any time consuming arguments ,and finally she ignored Phyllis' declaration only to evade embarrassment. Mrs. Price's actions stemmed from her desire to show authority even at the expense of poor Rachel who celebrated her eleventh birthday in the most awkward way. Rachel said it best, "Today I'm eleven. There's a cake Mama's making for tonight and when Papa comes home from work we'll eat it. There'll be candles and presents and everybody will sing Happy birthday, happy birthday to you, Rachel, only it's too late."

My Comments on Essay 3:

This essay is the best of the three essays. With minor style or language imperfections, this essay is very well written because:

- The writer divided the essay into 5 paragraphs.
- The writer clearly stated the reasons that made Mrs. Price act this way giving 3 solid hints on those reasons in the introduction.
- The writer quoted the passage in each of the 5 paragraphs to show his evidence.
- The writer used transitions well in all paragraphs (can you find them? Again.).
- The conclusion contains a summary of the points discussed in the body paragraphs.
- The introduction contains a scene setting sentence.
- The conclusion has a closing sentence taken from the passage.

A final note:

Remember to practice a lot. You can get more practice essays by emailing me any time. Good luck!

Bergen Academies Style Practice Sheet

The next fifteen questions are all questions that are almost identical in style and level (not format: the practice test in the following section is identical in format as well) to those you will see on the test.

Detailed explanations can be found after each question. Some or all of these questions have videos available online with detailed explanations. Please email me if you would the links to those videos.

1. If the sides of a square are increased by 30%, by what percentage will the area of the square increase?

A) 30% B) 60% C) 33% D) 120 % E) 69%

There are a few ways to answer this question. You can use some basic algebra or you can try to assume numbers and take it from there. Let's try the second approach.

Assume that the length of each side is 10 cm.

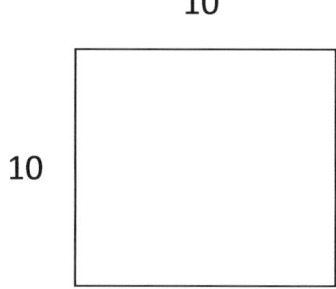

Area= 10 x 10 = 100 cm²

Now after increasing the length of the side by 30% each side becomes 13 cm.

The new area = 13 x 13= 169 cm²

Now you can see that the difference between the new and old areas is 69 cm².

Compare this difference to the original area. The difference is 69 and the original area is 100. Therefore the percent increase is 69%. The answer E.

2. A circular clock has the numbers 1 through 24 evenly spaced around it. Which of the following answers include the number that is directly across from 7?

A) 16 or 17   B) 18 or 19   C) 20 or 21   D) 5   E) 2

Just draw a circle (clock) and multiply each number on the clock by 2 because this strange clock has the numbers 1 through 24 evenly spaced around it instead of 1 to 12 like any regular clock. So 12 will be 24, 3 will be 6, 6 will be 12, and 9 will be 18.

Now check which number is directly across from 7. Please note that "directly across" means horizontally across not passing through the center of the circle (not a diameter).

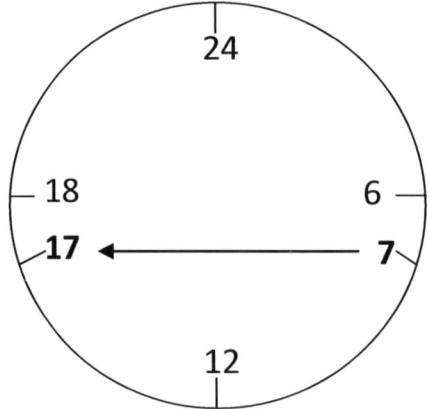

Right across of 7 is the number 17. A is the answer.

3. I want to cut a large slice of pizza into 4 equal pieces. If each cut takes 2 seconds, how many seconds will I need to get the job done?

A) 8   B) 6   C) 4   D) 2   E) 0.5

After 1 cut, your slice will be divided into 2 parts. After 2 cuts, you have 3 pieces. After 3 cuts, you now have 4 pieces. So to get 4 equal pieces, you need to make 3 cuts.

Since each cut takes 2 seconds, then the 3 cuts will take 6 seconds. The answer is B.

Note:

If the problem said "pizza" instead of "slice of pizza" you would only need 2 cuts: one vertical and one horizontal.

4. A clock loses 2 seconds every minute. How much time, in hours, must pass before this clock displays the correct time again?

A) 30   B) 60   C) 700   D) 720   E) 120

Let's start from the end:

For the clock to display the correct time again it must lose 24 whole hours to go back to its original time.

Now we need to figure out how much time (real time) must pass for that clock to lose 24 hours.

The clock loses:

2 seconds every 1 minute.

1 minute (2 seconds x 30) every 30 minutes (1 x 30 minutes).

1 hour (1 minute x 60)   every 30 hours (30 minutes x 60 = 1800 minutes = 30 hours).

24 hours (1 hour x 24)   every 720 hours (30 hours x 24 = 720 hours)

Therefore 720 hours or 30 days must pass for the clock to lose 24 hours. The answer is 720 hours. The answer is D.

5. A train is 90 meters long and enters a 310 meter long tunnel at a speed of 4 m/s. How much time in seconds will the train take to pass completely through the tunnel?

A) 90   B) 100   C) 400   D) 60   E) 360

For the train to pass completely through the tunnel it will travel 400 meters. Why you say?

Because for the train to pass "completely" means that the whole train must get "out" of the tunnel so the distance will be the length of the tunnel (at this point the front of the train is at the end of the tunnel but the rest of the train is still inside) + the length of the train (the distance needed for the whole train to get out of the tunnel).

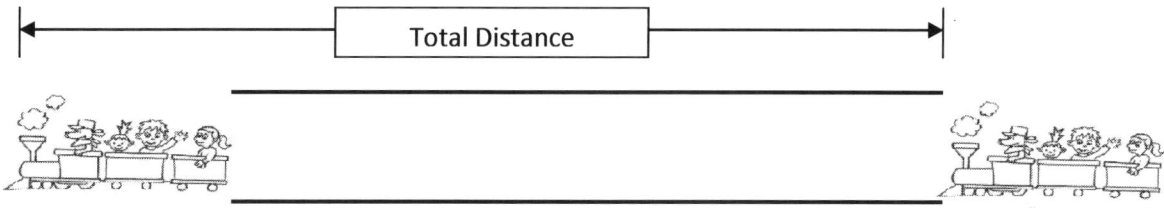

This means that the total distance is 310 m + 90 m which equals 400 m.

Since we know that Speed = Distance/Time

So

Time = Distance/ Speed

Since distance = 400 m and speed = 4 m/s (given)

Therefore Time = 400/4 = 100 seconds. The answer is B.

6. The average age of five boys is 15 years. A sixth boy joins them, making the average age 15 years and 6 months. What is the age of this sixth boy?

A) 15   B) 16   C) 18   D) 17   E) 14

OK. A classic "average" (sometimes called *arithmetic mean*) question. Let's remember the rule:

$$\text{Average} = \frac{\text{Sum of terms}}{\text{Number of terms}}$$

Let's take the first part: 5 boys whose average age is 15.

$$15 = \frac{\text{Sum of ages of the 5 boys}}{5}$$

Therefore, the Sum of ages of the 5 boys = 15 x 5 = 75 years

Now, the second part: 6 boys whose new average age is 15.5 (15 years and 6 months).

$$15.5 = \frac{\text{Sum of ages of the 6 boys}}{6}$$

$$15.5 = \frac{\text{Sum of ages of the first 5 boys} + \text{The age of boy 6}}{6}$$

$15.5 = \frac{75 + \text{Age of boy 6}}{6}$ Multiply both sides by 6

$15.5 \times 6 = 75 + \text{Age of Boy 6}$

$93 = 75 + \text{Age of boy 6}$ Subtract 75 from both sides

Age of boy 6 = 18 years. The answer is C.

7. What is the largest possible number of 10 cm X 8 cm cards that can be cut from a 90 cm x 30 cm sheet.

A) 30 B) 31 C) 32 D) 33 E) 34

The easiest and fastest way to answer this question is to divide the area of the large rectangle by the area of the small rectangle.

$$\frac{30 \times 90}{8 \times 10}$$

$$\frac{2700}{80}$$

The answer is 33.75 cards. We can't count 0.75 of a card as a complete card. So the answer is 33 cards only.

The answer is D.

Note:

This type of question is very popular on the BCA test.

8. 2 boys can eat 2 slices of pizza in 3 minutes. In how many minutes can 178 boys eat 178 slices of pizza?

   A) 178   B) 356   C) 534   D) 6   E) 3

Another popular type of question. Now:

2 boys   2 slices   3 minutes   Now think……..

3 boys   3 slices   ? minutes

Hmm……… 3 minutes. Why? Because each boy eats 1 slice in 3 minutes so 2 boys will eat two slices in 3 minutes and a hundred boys will eat a hundred slices in 3 minutes as well.

Therefore 178 boys can eat 178 slices in 3 minutes.

The answer is A.

9. A certain type of chocolate is sold only in 10 ounce boxes, costing $1.5 per box. How much will it cost to buy 2 pounds of this chocolate? There are 16 ounces in one pound.

A) $4.80   B) $6   C) $15   D) $3   E) $24

Now, 2 pounds of chocolate = 32 ounces (2 pounds x 16 ounces per pound)

Since this chocolate is only sold in 10 ounce boxes, then we must buy 4 boxes (40 ounces) although we only need 32 ounces (because 3 boxes will only give us 30 ounces).

4 boxes will cost $6 (4 x $1.5). The answer is B.

10. Evaluate the following:

$$\dfrac{1+\dfrac{3}{5}}{1+\dfrac{1}{1-\dfrac{1}{4}}}$$

A) $\dfrac{35}{24}$ B) $\dfrac{32}{24}$ C) $\dfrac{24}{35}$ D) $\dfrac{24}{32}$ E) 1

This is a popular and easy question just take it one step of a time.

$\dfrac{1+3/5}{1+1/(1-\frac{1}{4})} =$ (note: change the 1's to fractions)

$\dfrac{5/5+3/5}{1+1/(\frac{4}{4}-\frac{1}{4})} =$

$\dfrac{8/5}{1+1/(\frac{3}{4})} =$ (note: remember reciprocals)

$\dfrac{8/5}{1+\frac{4}{3}} =$

$\dfrac{8/5}{\frac{3}{3}+\frac{4}{3}} = \dfrac{8/5}{7/3} = \dfrac{8}{5} \times \dfrac{3}{7} = 24/35$. The answer is C.

11. The ratio of John's age to his son Adam's age is 8:3. If the sum of their ages is 55 years, what is the age difference between Adam and his dad in years?

A) 20   B) 25   C) 30   D) 35   E) 40

Most ratio questions on the test look like this. Write the given ratios and their total like this:

John's Age : Adam's Age : 55 (Total Age)

       8   :   3   :   11

The question is asking for the difference in their ages. From the proportion, the difference is 5 (8-3).

Now write a new proportion

Difference in Age (required) : 55 (Total Age)

            5   :   11

Remember from our chapter on proportions, cross multiply to find the missing part. Therefore:

The difference in age = $\frac{5 \times 55}{11} = 25$ years

The answer is B.

12. If A @ B means 2A – 3B, calculate the value of

   (2 @ 1) + (3 @ 2) ?

   A) 5   B) 8   C) 6   D) 1   E) 3

We know that A @ B = 2A – 3B so let's find the value of each of the two expressions (2 @ 1) & (3 @ 2).

1. (2 @ 1) = 2 x 2 – 3 x 1 = 1.

2. (3 @ 2) = 2 x 3 – 3 x 2 = 0.

So (2 @ 1) + (3 @ 2) = 1 + 0 = 1. The answer is D.

13. A room is now half full, if it becomes a quarter full after 35 people leave the room, how many people does the room hold when it is full?

A) 35   B) 70   C) 140   D) 210   E) 280

This room was half full then it became a quarter full after 35 people left. We know that a quarter full is half of "half full". This means that that the 35 people resemble a quarter of the people making the room full.

Therefore, the full capacity of the room is:

4 x 35 = 140 people. The answer is C.

14. If you multiply the product of all the integers from -15 to 4 by the sum of the first 50 positive odd numbers, the answer is?

A) -3000   B) 3000   C) 0   D) -55   E) 60

Now, remember that 0 is an integer. Also, remember that multiplying any number of integers that include the number 0 will always give a product of 0.

This means that "the product of all the integers from -15 to 4" equals zero.

Therefore 0 multiplied by "the sum of the first 50 positive odd numbers" **or anything else for that matter equals zero.**

The answer is C.

15. Which of the following numbers is the closest answer to the square root of 20 million?

A) 20000   B) 10000   C) 4000   D) 4500   E) 5000

Remember from our chapter *See You Later Calculator* that any even number of zeros under a square root will be translated into half that number of zeros outside the square root.

Ex: $\sqrt{40000} = 200$

Now, back to our question:

$\sqrt{20,000,000} = \sqrt{20} \times 1000$

We know that $\sqrt{25} = 5$

We know that $\sqrt{16} = 4$

Therefore $\sqrt{20}$ **equals approximately 4.5.**

Then the answer is approximately 4.5 x 1000 = 4500.

The answer is D.

Answers

1. E
2. A
3. B
4. D
5. B
6. C
7. D
8. E
9. B
10. C
11. B
12. D
13. C
14. C
15. D

Bergen County Academies Sample Test

This test resembles the math portion of the Bergen County Academies entrance exam.

You have exactly sixty minutes to complete the 40-question test.

Two points are given for each correct answer and one-half point is deducted for each incorrect answer. Unanswered questions are not counted.

Detailed videos answering each question on this test are available. Please send an email to kareem@kareemgouda.com requesting links to these videos.

USE OF CALCULATORS IS NOT ALLOWED

The answers are:
01 - 10   E B B D D E C E C C
11 - 20   C A E B E E B E D C
21 - 30   C E B A B E D A A D
31 - 40   B D E E C D C D C B

1. A gallon of water weighs 8 pounds. It takes 10 pounds of water to make a pound of sauce. How many pounds of sauce can be made from 4 gallons of water? Round your answer to the nearest pound.

   A 2   B 7   C 5   D 8   E 3

2. What is the area, in square miles, of a square shaped plot of land with a perimeter of 8 miles?

   A 64   B 4   C 8   D 12   E 16

3. How many positive factors, including 1 and itself does 52 have?

   A 4   B 6   C 8
   D 12 E 16

4. Calculate the following:

   $(0.4)^2 - (-0.2)^2 =$

   A 0.2   B 0.4   C -0.8   D 0.12   E -0.16

5. Jenny got 70% on a 20-problem test, 80% on a 40-problem test, and 90% on a 60 problem test. If all three tests are combined into one 120-problem test, what is her percent score, given to the nearest whole percent?

   A 79%   B 80%   C 82%   D 83%   E 85%

6. Other than 2 and 15, how many whole positive numbers divide evenly into 60?

   A 6   B 7   C 8   D 9   E 10

7. Find the difference if the sum of the first 73 positive integers is subtracted from the sum of the first 74 positive integers.

   A 1   B 73   C 74   D 147   E 0

8. If 2/3 of a number is 48, what is 3/4 of that number?

   A 24   B 44   C 36   D 52   E 54

9. How many ninths are in 5.75?

   A 54   B 44   C 51   D 52   E 54

10. Calculate the value of:

    $(0.2)^3 =$

    A 0.8   B 0.08   C 0.008
    D 0.0008   E 0.00008

11. One day from 10:52 AM to 1:36PM, a group of painters began to paint some paintings at a competition. At what time was the competition half over?

   A 12:10 B 12:13 C 12:14 D 12:20 E 12:25

12. How many two-digit numbers consist of two even digits?

   A <26 B 26 C 27 D 28 E >28

13. What is the largest sum which can be obtained by adding a negative integer to its reciprocal?

   A -5.2 B -4.25 C -3.3 D -2.5 E 0

14. A toy store increases its prices by 10% and then decreases the new prices of their toys by 10%. What is the price of an originally $50 toy after the two changes?

   A $49.20   B $49.50   C $50.00
   D. $50.50 E $49.80

15. Determine the value of the following expression:

   $$[(-4)(2) - (-2)] \div 3/6$$

   A -5 B 12 C 5 D 20 E -12

16. The postage rate for first class mail is 46¢ for the first ounce and 17¢ for each additional ounce or fraction of an ounce. How much will it cost to send a 5½ ounce package by first class mail?

   A <63¢   B 63¢ to 79¢   C 88¢ to 99¢
   D $1.00 to $1.20   E >$1.25

17. The average of 2/4, 6/9, and 6/8 is:

   A 2/3   B 23/36   C 22/13
   D 23/25   E 5/12

18. Which of the following fractions is equal to 2%?

   A 5/4 B 5/40 C 1/80 D 4/500 E 1/50

19. How many numbers between 3 and 101 are exactly divisible by 4?

   A 22 B 23 C 24 D 25 E 26

20. What is 2% of 1/2?

   A 0.4   B 0.001   C 0.01
   D 0.0001 E 0.00004

21. Suppose 60 is divided into 3 parts in the ratio of 1:3:6. What is the value of the middle part?

   A 60   B 30   C 18   D 20   E 3

22. Which of the following is closest to 0.5?

   A 19/40   B 7/16   C 15/32   D 0.4   E 31/64

23. The announcement read "Buy 3 phones at the regular price and get any more phones for only half the price." John paid $320 for 5 phones. What is the regular price of a phone?

   A $85   B $80   C $90   D $95   E $100

24. If A @ B means (A + B) x 1/2, then (3 @ 5) @ 8 =

   A 6   B 8   C 4   D 12   E 16

25. Blue and yellow paint are mixed to make green paint. If the amount of blue paint needed is half the amount of yellow paint, how many gallons of blue paint are needed to make 10 gallons of green paint? Round to the nearest gallon.

   A 2   B 3   C 4   D 5   E 6

26. When the number halfway between 2/16 and 7/12 is added to 1, the answer is:

   A 17/48   B 5/12   C 5/16   D 11/48   E 65/48

27. What is the value of the largest 2-digit positive integer whose digits have a product of 9?

   A <30   B 33 to 39   C 40 to 80   D 91 to 95   E >95

28. What is the 45th term in the series which starts 3, 6, 9, 12.......?

   A 135   B 120   C 124   D 45   E 137

29. Which of the following is closest to 2?

   A 2.009   B 2.011   C 198/100
   D 200/99   E $2 - \frac{1}{101}$

30. Jen spent 1/5 of her raise on food, 1/4 on gas and 1/3 on clothes. She then spent her final 13 dollars on a present. How much is Jen's raise?

   A 156   B 158   C 70   D 60   E 68

31. Kim has a job at the candy factory. Each day she is paid 5 cents each for the first 50 candies she makes, 8 cents each for the next 30 candies and 9 cents each for any additional candies. How many candies must she make, in one hour, to earn $6.70?

   A 110   B 100   C 120   D 156   E 177

32. Four circles are to be drawn along the center line of a square shaped sheet of paper so that their centers are 2.2 inches apart. The centers of the end circles are to be 1.7 inches from their respective ends. What is the area of this sheet of paper in square inches?

   A 64   B 81   C 90   D 100   E 121

33. Multiplying by 3/4 and then dividing by 3/7 is the same as multiplying by what?

   A 11/3   B 6/7   C 4/7   D 6/28   E 7/4

34. Jim brought some candies to the fundraiser. Dan bought 1/10 of them and Sue bought 1/4 of the remaining candies. If Dan bought 12 candies, how many candies did Jim have left after Dan and Sue left?

   A 77   B 78   C 79   D 80   E 81

35. To make 5 dozen cookies I need 3 cups of flour, 2 cup of butter, 2½ cups of sugar and 3 eggs. How many cookies can I make if I have 9 cups of flour, 3 cups of butter, 5 cups of sugar and 6 eggs?

   A 180   B 36   C 90   D 120   E 60

36. If it is now 3:00 PM. What time will it be 1000 hours from now?

   A 7:00 PM   B 11:00 AM   C 2:00 PM
   D 7:00 AM   E 11:00 PM

37. The value of one British pound is 30% more than the value of one American dollar. A British tourist visiting New Jersey wants to buy a souvenir that costs $36 with fifty British pounds. If the store accepts British pounds, what should be her change, in American dollars?

   A $13.30   B $14   C $29
   D $12   E $25

38. A rectangle whose width is 5 inches has the same area as a square whose side is 10 inches. What is the perimeter of this rectangle?

   A 25   B 30   C 100   D 50   E 53

39. A clock loses 1 second every 5 minutes. It is set to the correct time at 8 PM on May 7. In which month is the next day on which it shows the correct time?

   A January   B February   C March   D April   E May

40. How many positive factors of 36 are also multiples of both 2 and 3?

   A 3   B 4   C 5   D 6   E 7

Basic Math Concepts Practice Sheets Chapter by chapter

The following questions are arranged by chapter. Some of these questions, though seemingly easy, do appear on the BCA test. Other questions are provided for practice on the main topics that are tested on the BCA test.

Answers for each practice sheet are provided after each sheet.

Math Practice by Kareem Gouda   www.SKOOLOO.com

Chapter 1 Questions: Place Value

Write the name of each place indicated.

1) <u>4</u>,846,790

2) <u>1</u>12

3) <u>5</u>4

4) 8,444,<u>3</u>66

5) 5<u>3</u>,016,607

6) 17,5<u>8</u>8,917

7) 2,97<u>1</u>,159

8) 3,4<u>7</u>1

9) 3,006,70<u>3</u>

10) 81<u>6</u>,578,025

11) 1,<u>2</u>55

12) 6,<u>6</u>05,577

13) 60,<u>1</u>78,809

14) 5,540,<u>0</u>21

15) 203,<u>1</u>63

16) 7<u>5</u>

17) <u>9</u>,167,715

18) 83<u>0</u>,927

19) 90,2<u>9</u>2,269

20) 835,<u>7</u>65,580

21) 7,8<u>1</u>2

22) 89<u>2</u>,032

23) 64,3<u>6</u>4

24) 4,<u>9</u>57,686

25) <u>9</u>,828

26) 88<u>1</u>,930

27) <u>8</u>,554,270

28) 58<u>2</u>

29) 17,<u>4</u>99,724

30) 72,851,0<u>3</u>6

31) 7,5<u>2</u>4,378

32) 471,<u>8</u>20

33) <u>1</u>6,690

34) 47<u>3</u>

35) 8<u>1</u>,143,142

36) 28<u>0</u>,088,695

37) <u>3</u>,047

38) 40,<u>7</u>37

39) 8̲5,389

40) 5,730,8̲33

41) 258,59̲1

42) 3,155̲

43) 8̲77,385

44) 99,340̲,607

45) 2̲74,251

46) 54,702,9̲39

47) 847,493̲

48) 309̲,505

49) 4̲5

50) 46̲4,156

Answers to Chapter 1 Questions: Place Value

1) millions
2) hundreds
3) tens
4) hundreds
5) millions
6) ten thousands
7) thousands
8) tens
9) ones
10) millions
11) hundreds
12) hundred thousands
13) hundred thousands
14) hundreds
15) hundreds
16) ones
17) millions
18) thousands
19) ten thousands
20) hundred thousands
21) tens
22) thousands
23) tens
24) hundred thousands
25) thousands
26) thousands
27) millions
28) ones
29) thousands
30) tens
31) ten thousands
32) hundreds
33) ten thousands
34) ones
35) millions
36) millions
37) thousands
38) hundreds
39) ten thousands
40) hundreds
41) tens
42) ones
43) hundred thousands
44) thousands
45) hundred thousands
46) hundreds
47) ones
48) thousands
49) tens
50) ten thousands

Math Practice by Kareem Gouda www.SKOOLOO.com

Chapter 1 Questions: Rounding Numbers

Round each number to the place indicated.

1) 2,9_2_6,276

2) 45,8_9_9,496

3) 251,_9_28

4) _9_0

5) 398,_2_82

6) 6_0_,594

7) 10,523,_8_36

8) 5_5_,915,146

9) _4_88,187

10) 7_3_1

11) _4_9

12) 84,98_5_,053

13) 629,6_5_8,283

14) _5_05

15) 52_8_,582,847

16) 7,05_9_.2

17) 9,649,39_1_.4

18) 2,102,_6_01

19) 7_4_,943

20) 2_4_7,955

21) 9,2_9_7

22) 5_1_9

23) 4,740._0_6

24) 6,_9_60

25) 79_9_,392

26) 300,3_9_3,614

27) _8_36,856

28) _8_.7

29) _8_.9

30) 33,7_1_0

31) 7_5_,806,752

32) 30,57_9_,074

33) 4,_9_51,306

34) 9_9_5,858

35) 64_9_,423,526

36) 48,55_9_,170

37) 22,4_0_2

38) 5,_6_23

157

39) 294,1<u>6</u>7,965

40) 5<u>7</u>,520,275

41) <u>9</u>,092,517

42) 785,5<u>2</u>9

43) 3,1<u>5</u>7,861

44) 56,619,<u>9</u>83

45) 282,<u>3</u>13

46) 7<u>5</u>4,635

47) 2<u>9</u>,219,967

48) <u>9</u>.9

49) 354,42<u>1</u>.1

50) 6,7<u>4</u>6,731

Answers to Chapter 1 Questions: Rounding Numbers

1) 2,900,000
2) 45,900,000
3) 251,900
4) 90
5) 398,300
6) 61,000
7) 10,523,800
8) 56,000,000
9) 500,000
10) 730
11) 50
12) 84,985,000
13) 629,660,000
14) 500
15) 529,000,000
16) 7,059
17) 9,649,391
18) 2,102,600
19) 75,000
20) 250,000
21) 9,300
22) 520
23) 4,741
24) 7,000
25) 799,000
26) 300,390,000
27) 800,000
28) 9
29) 9
30) 33,710
31) 76,000,000
32) 30,579,000
33) 5,000,000
34) 1,000,000
35) 649,000,000
36) 48,559,000
37) 22,400
38) 5,600
39) 294,170,000
40) 58,000,000
41) 9,000,000
42) 785,530
43) 3,160,000
44) 56,620,000
45) 282,300
46) 750,000
47) 29,000,000
48) 10
49) 354,421
50) 6,750,000

Math Practice by Kareem Gouda   www.SKOOLOO.com

Chapter 1 Questions: Divisibility

State if the first number is divisible by the second number.

1) 142 by 3   2) 147 by 6

3) 144 by 6   4) 74 by 2

5) 77 by 5   6) 80 by 6

7) 80 by 10   8) 87 by 3

9) 90 by 5   10) 90 by 9

11) 96 by 3   12) 100 by 3

13) 107 by 6   14) 106 by 2

15) 110 by 2   16) 118 by 6

17) 114 by 10   18) 120 by 10

19) 120 by 5   20) 126 by 9

21) 130 by 10   22) 132 by 3

23) 137 by 6   24) 135 by 9

25) 142 by 2   26) 152 by 6

27) 79 by 10   28) 80 by 5

29) 90 by 3   30) 92 by 9

31) 100 by 2   32) 102 by 6

33) 111 by 2   34) 113 by 5

35) 115 by 5   36) 125 by 5

37) 123 by 3   38) 132 by 2

39) 135 by 3

40) 138 by 6

41) 147 by 2

42) 148 by 5

43) 70 by 10

44) 81 by 9

45) 85 by 9

46) 93 by 3

47) 96 by 6

48) 99 by 9

49) 102 by 2

50) 109 by 5

Answers to Chapter 1 Questions: Divisibility

1) No	2) No	3) Yes
4) Yes	5) No	6) No
7) Yes	8) Yes	9) Yes
10) Yes	11) Yes	12) No
13) No	14) Yes	15) Yes
16) No	17) No	18) Yes
19) Yes	20) Yes	21) Yes
22) Yes	23) No	24) Yes
25) Yes	26) No	27) No
28) Yes	29) Yes	30) No
31) Yes	32) Yes	33) No
34) No	35) Yes	36) Yes
37) Yes	38) Yes	39) Yes
40) Yes	41) No	42) No
43) Yes	44) Yes	45) No
46) Yes	47) Yes	48) Yes
49) Yes	50) No	

Chapter 1 Questions: Factorization

List all positive factors of each.

1) 53

2) 56

3) 60

4) 63

5) 66

6) 73

7) 69

8) 76

9) 79

10) 83

11) 86

12) 89

13) 92

14) 96

15) 99

16) 51

17) 54

18) 58

19) 61

20) 64

21) 67

22) 74

23) 71

24) 77

25) 81

26) 84

27) 87

28) 90

29) 94

30) 97

31) 100

32) 52

33) 59

34) 62

35) 65

36) 72

37) 75

38) 82

39) 85

40) 88

41) 95

42) 98

43) 50

44) 57

45) 70

46) 80

47) 93

48) 55

49) 68

50) 78

Answers to Chapter 1 Questions: Factorization

1) 1, 53
2) 1, 2, 4, 7, 8, 14, 28, 56
3) 1, 2, 3, 4, 5, 6, 10, 12, 15, 20, 30, 60
4) 1, 3, 7, 9, 21, 63
5) 1, 2, 3, 6, 11, 22, 33, 66
6) 1, 73
7) 1, 3, 23, 69
8) 1, 2, 4, 19, 38, 76
9) 1, 79
10) 1, 83
11) 1, 2, 43, 86
12) 1, 89
13) 1, 2, 4, 23, 46, 92
14) 1, 2, 3, 4, 6, 8, 12, 16, 24, 32, 48, 96
15) 1, 3, 9, 11, 33, 99
16) 1, 3, 17, 51
17) 1, 2, 3, 6, 9, 18, 27, 54
18) 1, 2, 29, 58
19) 1, 61
20) 1, 2, 4, 8, 16, 32, 64
21) 1, 67
22) 1, 2, 37, 74
23) 1, 71
24) 1, 7, 11, 77
25) 1, 3, 9, 27, 81
26) 1, 2, 3, 4, 6, 7, 12, 14, 21, 28, 42, 84
27) 1, 3, 29, 87
28) 1, 2, 3, 5, 6, 9, 10, 15, 18, 30, 45, 90
29) 1, 2, 47, 94
30) 1, 97
31) 1, 2, 4, 5, 10, 20, 25, 50, 100
32) 1, 2, 4, 13, 26, 52
33) 1, 59
34) 1, 2, 31, 62
35) 1, 5, 13, 65
36) 1, 2, 3, 4, 6, 8, 9, 12, 18, 24, 36, 72
37) 1, 3, 5, 15, 25, 75
38) 1, 2, 41, 82
39) 1, 5, 17, 85
40) 1, 2, 4, 8, 11, 22, 44, 88
41) 1, 5, 19, 95
42) 1, 2, 7, 14, 49, 98
43) 1, 2, 5, 10, 25, 50
44) 1, 3, 19, 57
45) 1, 2, 5, 7, 10, 14, 35, 70
46) 1, 2, 4, 5, 8, 10, 16, 20, 40, 80
47) 1, 3, 31, 93
48) 1, 5, 11, 55
49) 1, 2, 4, 17, 34, 68
50) 1, 2, 3, 6, 13, 26, 39, 78

Chapter 1 Questions: Prime Factorization

Write the prime factorization of each. Do not use exponents.

1) 84

2) 81

3) 91

4) 88

5) 94

6) 97

7) 50

8) 53

9) 56

10) 59

11) 63

12) 66

13) 72

14) 69

15) 76

16) 79

17) 86

18) 89

19) 82

20) 92

21) 95

22) 99

23) 51

24) 57

25) 54

26) 61

27) 67

28) 64

29) 74

30) 70

31) 77

32) 80

33) 87

34) 90

35) 93

36) 100

37) 52

38) 55

39) 62 40) 65

41) 68 42) 75

43) 78 44) 85

45) 98 46) 60

47) 73 48) 83

49) 96 50) 58

Answers to Chapter 1 Questions: Prime Factorization

1) $2 \cdot 2 \cdot 3 \cdot 7$
2) $3 \cdot 3 \cdot 3 \cdot 3$
3) $7 \cdot 13$
4) $2 \cdot 2 \cdot 2 \cdot 11$
5) $2 \cdot 47$
6) 97
7) $2 \cdot 5 \cdot 5$
8) 53
9) $2 \cdot 2 \cdot 2 \cdot 7$
10) 59
11) $3 \cdot 3 \cdot 7$
12) $2 \cdot 3 \cdot 11$
13) $2 \cdot 2 \cdot 2 \cdot 3 \cdot 3$
14) $3 \cdot 23$
15) $2 \cdot 2 \cdot 19$
16) 79
17) $2 \cdot 43$
18) 89
19) $2 \cdot 41$
20) $2 \cdot 2 \cdot 23$
21) $5 \cdot 19$
22) $3 \cdot 3 \cdot 11$
23) $3 \cdot 17$
24) $3 \cdot 19$
25) $2 \cdot 3 \cdot 3 \cdot 3$
26) 61
27) 67
28) $2 \cdot 2 \cdot 2 \cdot 2 \cdot 2 \cdot 2$
29) $2 \cdot 37$
30) $2 \cdot 5 \cdot 7$
31) $7 \cdot 11$
32) $2 \cdot 2 \cdot 2 \cdot 2 \cdot 5$
33) $3 \cdot 29$
34) $2 \cdot 3 \cdot 3 \cdot 5$
35) $3 \cdot 31$
36) $2 \cdot 2 \cdot 5 \cdot 5$
37) $2 \cdot 2 \cdot 13$
38) $5 \cdot 11$
39) $2 \cdot 31$
40) $5 \cdot 13$
41) $2 \cdot 2 \cdot 17$
42) $3 \cdot 5 \cdot 5$
43) $2 \cdot 3 \cdot 13$
44) $5 \cdot 17$
45) $2 \cdot 7 \cdot 7$
46) $2 \cdot 2 \cdot 3 \cdot 5$
47) 73
48) 83
49) $2 \cdot 2 \cdot 2 \cdot 2 \cdot 2 \cdot 3$
50) $2 \cdot 29$

Math Practice by KareemGouda	www.SKOOLOO.com

Chapter 1 Questions: Multiplying Numbers with Exponents

Use the rule for multiplying numbers with exponents to find the answer. Remember: Add the powers.

1) $3 \cdot 3^2$ 2) $2^2 \cdot 2^2$

3) $2 \cdot 2^2 \cdot 2^2$ 4) $3 \cdot 3^3 \cdot 3^2$

5) $6 \cdot 6^3 \cdot 6^3$ 6) $2^3 \cdot 2^2 \cdot 2^2$

7) $3 \cdot 3^3$ 8) $2 \cdot 2^3$

9) $5 \cdot 5^3$ 10) $5^3 \cdot 5^2$

11) $4^3 \cdot 4^2$ 12) $3 \cdot 3^2$

13) $6 \cdot 6^2$ 14) $2 \cdot 2^2$

15) $3^2 \cdot 3^2$ 16) $2^3 \cdot 2^3$

17) $3^3 \cdot 3^3$ 18) $4^3 \cdot 4^3$

19) $2 \cdot 2^3$ 20) $3 \cdot 3^3$

21) $2 \cdot 2^2$ 22) $4 \cdot 4^2$

23) $4 \cdot 4^3$ 24) $5^3 \cdot 5^3$

25) $5 \cdot 5^3 \cdot 5^3$ 26) $5^3 \cdot 5^2 \cdot 5^3$

27) $4 \cdot 4^3 \cdot 4^2$ 28) $6^2 \cdot 6^3 \cdot 6^2$

29) $2^2 \cdot 2^3$ 30) $3^2 \cdot 3^3$

31) $6^2 \cdot 6^3$ 32) $5 \cdot 5^3$

33) $3^3 \cdot 3^2$ 34) $2^3 \cdot 2^2$

35) $5^2 \cdot 5^2$ 36) $6^3 \cdot 6^3$

37) $4 \cdot 2^3$ 38) $6 \cdot 6^2$

39) $4 \cdot 4^2$ 40) $2 \cdot 2^3 \cdot 2^3$

41) $4^2 \cdot 4^3 \cdot 4^2$ 42) $2 \cdot 2^3 \cdot 2^3$

43) $5 \cdot 5^2 \cdot 5^2$ 44) $6^3 \cdot 6^2 \cdot 6^3$

45) $5 \cdot 5^2$ 46) $6 \cdot 6^3$

47) $4^2 \cdot 4^2$ 48) $6^2 \cdot 6^2$

49) $4 \cdot 4^3$ 50) $4^3 \cdot 4^3 \cdot 4^2$

Answers to Chapter 1 Questions: Multiplying Numbers with Exponents

1) 3^3
2) 2^4
3) 2^5
4) 3^6
5) 6^7
6) 2^7
7) 3^4
8) 2^4
9) 5^4
10) 5^5
11) 4^5
12) 3^3
13) 6^3
14) 2^3
15) 3^4
16) 2^6
17) 3^6
18) 4^6
19) 2^4
20) 3^4
21) 2^3
22) 4^3
23) 4^4
24) 5^6
25) 5^7
26) 5^8
27) 4^6
28) 6^7
29) 2^5
30) 3^5
31) 6^5
32) 5^4
33) 3^5
34) 2^5
35) 5^4
36) 6^6
37) 2^5
38) 6^3
39) 4^3
40) 2^7
41) 4^7
42) 2^7
43) 5^5
44) 6^8
45) 5^3
46) 6^4
47) 4^4
48) 6^4
49) 4^4
50) 4^8

Math Practice by KareemGouda   www.SKOOLOO.com

Chapter 1 Questions: Dividing Numbers with Exponents

Use the rule for dividing numbers with exponents to find the answer. Remember: Subtract the powers. Also note that a number with a negative exponent is the same as ONE OVER THAT NUMBER WITH A POSITIVE EXPONENT.

1) $\dfrac{10^3}{10}$

2) $\dfrac{6^3}{6^5}$

3) $\dfrac{10^5}{10^2}$

4) $\dfrac{6^2}{6^5}$

5) $\dfrac{8^2}{8^2}$

6) $\dfrac{4^2}{4^5}$

7) $\dfrac{9}{9^3}$

8) $\dfrac{3^4}{3^3}$

9) $\dfrac{2^4}{2^2}$

10) $\dfrac{10^5}{10}$

11) $\dfrac{4}{4^4}$

12) $\dfrac{8^3}{8}$

13) $\dfrac{7^3}{7^5}$

14) $\dfrac{2^5}{2^2}$

15) $\dfrac{8^5}{8^2}$

16) $\dfrac{6^2}{6}$

17) $\dfrac{9^2}{9^3}$

18) $\dfrac{5^4}{5^4}$

19) $\dfrac{5}{5}$

20) $\dfrac{10^4}{10^3}$

21) $\dfrac{4^3}{4}$

22) $\dfrac{3^3}{3^4}$

23) $\dfrac{9^3}{9^4}$

24) $\dfrac{2^5}{2^5}$

25) $\dfrac{6^5}{6^2}$

26) $\dfrac{8}{8^2}$

27) $\dfrac{7^4}{7^3}$

28) $\dfrac{3^3}{3}$

29) $\dfrac{10^3}{10^4}$

30) $\dfrac{4^3}{4^2}$

31) $\dfrac{10^2}{10^5}$

32) $\dfrac{5^5}{5^3}$

33) $\dfrac{2^4}{2}$

34) $\dfrac{7}{7^3}$

35) $\dfrac{10^4}{10}$

36) $\dfrac{7^3}{7^4}$

37) $\dfrac{8^3}{8^4}$

38) $\dfrac{2^5}{2^3}$

39) $\dfrac{4^4}{4}$

40) $\dfrac{5^4}{5^3}$

41) $\dfrac{5}{5^4}$

42) $\dfrac{9^3}{9}$

43) $\dfrac{5^3}{5^4}$

44) $\dfrac{10^3}{10^2}$

45) $\dfrac{10}{10^3}$

46) $\dfrac{6^3}{6^2}$

47) $\dfrac{3}{3^4}$

48) $\dfrac{4^2}{4}$

49) $\dfrac{7^4}{7}$

50) $\dfrac{9^2}{9^4}$

Answers to Chapter 1 Questions: Dividing Numbers with Exponents

1) 10^2

2) $\dfrac{1}{6^2}$

3) 10^3

4) $\dfrac{1}{6^3}$

5) 1

6) $\dfrac{1}{4^3}$

7) $\dfrac{1}{9^2}$

8) 3

9) 2^2

10) 10^4

11) $\dfrac{1}{4^3}$

12) 8^2

13) $\dfrac{1}{7^2}$

14) 2^3

15) 8^3

16) 6

17) $\dfrac{1}{9}$

18) 1

19) 1

20) 10

21) 4^2

22) $\dfrac{1}{3}$

23) $\dfrac{1}{9}$

24) 1

25) 6^3

26) $\dfrac{1}{8}$

27) 7

28) 3^2

29) $\dfrac{1}{10}$

30) 4

31) $\dfrac{1}{10^3}$

32) 5^2

33) 2^3

34) $\dfrac{1}{7^2}$

35) 10^3

36) $\dfrac{1}{7}$

37) $\dfrac{1}{8}$

38) 2^2

39) 4^3

40) 5

41) $\dfrac{1}{5^3}$

42) 9^2

43) $\dfrac{1}{5}$

44) 10

45) $\dfrac{1}{10^2}$

46) 6

47) $\dfrac{1}{3^3}$

48) 4

49) 7^3

50) $\dfrac{1}{9^2}$

Chapter 1 Questions: Square Roots

Find each square root.

1) $\sqrt{400}$

2) $\sqrt{0}$

3) $\sqrt{9}$

4) $\sqrt{49}$

5) $\sqrt{100}$

6) $\sqrt{169}$

7) $\sqrt{256}$

8) $\sqrt{36}$

9) $\sqrt{361}$

10) $\sqrt{81}$

11) $\sqrt{484}$

12) $\sqrt{144}$

13) $\sqrt{4}$

14) $\sqrt{225}$

15) $\sqrt{25}$

16) $\sqrt{324}$

17) $\sqrt{64}$

18) $\sqrt{441}$

19) $\sqrt{324}$

20) $\sqrt{441}$

21) $\sqrt{576}$

22) $\sqrt{729}$

23) $\sqrt{961}$

24) $\sqrt{4}$

25) $\sqrt{25}$

26) $\sqrt{81}$

27) $\sqrt{144}$

28) $\sqrt{225}$

29) $\sqrt{484}$

30) $\sqrt{625}$

31) $\sqrt{784}$

32) $\sqrt{9}$

33) $\sqrt{36}$

34) $\sqrt{256}$

35) $\sqrt{361}$

36) $\sqrt{676}$

37) $\sqrt{841}$

38) $\sqrt{0}$

39) $\sqrt{49}$

41) $\sqrt{169}$

43) $\sqrt{529}$

45) $\sqrt{1}$

47) $\sqrt{196}$

49) $\sqrt{900}$

40) $\sqrt{100}$

42) $\sqrt{400}$

44) $\sqrt{16}$

46) $\sqrt{121}$

48) $\sqrt{289}$

50) $\sqrt{64}$

Answers to Chapter 1 Questions: Square Roots

1) 20	2) 0	3) 3
4) 7	5) 10	6) 13
7) 16	8) 6	9) 19
10) 9	11) 22	12) 12
13) 2	14) 15	15) 5
16) 18	17) 8	18) 21
19) 18	20) 21	21) 24
22) 27	23) 31	24) 2
25) 5	26) 9	27) 12
28) 15	29) 22	30) 25
31) 28	32) 3	33) 6
34) 16	35) 19	36) 26
37) 29	38) 0	39) 7
40) 10	41) 13	42) 20
43) 23	44) 4	45) 1
46) 11	47) 14	48) 17
49) 30	50) 8	

Chapter 1 Questions: Order of Operations

Evaluate each expression using the order of operations.

1) $(24 + 4) \div (8 - (3 + 1))$

2) $((8 + 1) \times 2) \div (3 - 1)$

3) $((16 - 1) \times 2) \div (3 + 3)$

4) $(18 + 6 - 5 + 1) \div 5$

5) $(1 + 2 + 5 - 2) \div 6$

6) $(4 + 18 - 2) \div 2 + 4$

7) $6 - (12 - 3^2) \div 3$

8) $(3 - 8 \div 8)(2 + 8)$

9) $5 \times 10 \div (5 \times 2 - 8)$

10) $7 - 3 + 7 + 9 + 7$

11) $2^2 - 15 \div (2 + 3)$

12) $(15 + 11 - 9 + 1) \div 3$

13) $(2 + 7 - 5) \times 4 - 7$

14) $((22 - (2 - 1)) \times 3) \div 9$

15) $6 - (23 - 7) \div 2^3$

16) $9 + 2 - 6 - (9 - 7)$

17) $3 \times 8(5 - (1 + 2))$

18) $9 \times (9 \times 2 - 8) \div 10$

19) $3^2 \times 16 \div (5 - 3)$

20) $9 - (10 - (7 - 6) \times 2)$

21) $9 \times 27 \div (9 \times 1^2)$

22) $(3 + 6) \div 3 \times 18 \div 3$

23) $27 \div (7 \times 2 - (4 + 7))$

24) $9 + 5 - 10 + 6 - 3$

25) $(14 + 3 \times 2 - 10) \div 2$

26) $(8 - (2 - (8 - 7))) \div 7$

27) $(6 \times 2) \div 6$

28) $10 + 7 \times 7 - 7 \times 4$

29) $4 \times 3 + 1 + 9 + 4$

30) $7 - 3 + 2 + 7 + 8$

31) $21 \div 7 - 2 + 9 \div 3$

32) $2 \times 9 \times 5 + 8 \div 4$

33) $2 - (2 + 3) \div (6 - 1)$

34) $6 \times 3(2 + 2) - 5$

35) $8 - (5 + 3 + 1 - 9)$

36) $10 - (3 + 7 - 2) \div 8$

37) $(7 - 6)^3(3 - 2)$

38) $3 + 10 + 2 - 2 \times 3$

39) $8 - (5 \times 2) \div 5 + 8$

40) $9 - 6 + 8 + 3 \times 8$

41) $(1 + 8 - 6) \times 4 \times 3$

42) $10 \times 28 \div 4 + 2 - 1$

43) $(5 + 6 - (8 - 1)) \times 10$

44) $21 \div (10 - (6 - (5 - 2)))$

45) $(23 - 1 + 2) \div 3 - 2$

46) $(7 - 2)^2 - (2 + 4)$

47) $(27 \times 2) \div (9 - 6)^2$

48) $(25 - 9) \div ((4 - 3) \times 2)$

49) $(12 - 4 + 8) \div (3 - 1)$

50) $8 \div (6 - 4) + 3 + 2$

Answers to Chapter 1 Questions: Order of Operations

1) 7	2) 9	3) 5
4) 4	5) 1	6) 14
7) 5	8) 20	9) 25
10) 27	11) 1	12) 6
13) 9	14) 7	15) 4
16) 3	17) 48	18) 9
19) 72	20) 1	21) 27
22) 18	23) 9	24) 7
25) 5	26) 1	27) 2
28) 31	29) 26	30) 21
31) 4	32) 92	33) 1
34) 67	35) 8	36) 9
37) 1	38) 9	39) 14
40) 35	41) 36	42) 71
43) 40	44) 3	45) 6
46) 19	47) 6	48) 8
49) 8	50) 9	

Chapter 1: Absolute Value

What are the possible values of each letter inside the absolute value signs. Example: p, in question number 1, could be 7 or -7 because the absolute value of either would be 7.

1) $|p| = 7$

2) $|p| = 49$

3) $|n| = 15$

4) $|m| = 36$

5) $|r| = 41$

6) $|x| = 20$

7) $|n| = 24$

8) $|b| = 44$

9) $|x| = 12$

10) $|v| = 33$

11) $|x| = 9$

12) $|a| = 53$

13) $|k| = 47$

14) $|p| = 4$

15) $|x| = 17$

16) $|n| = 60$

17) $|m| = 39$

18) $|r| = 5$

19) $|n| = 52$

20) $|x| = 26$

21) $|b| = 31$

22) $|v| = 10$

23) $|x| = 34$

24) $|n| = 55$

25) $|a| = 22$

26) $|x| = 42$

27) $|k| = 2$

28) $|x| = 58$

29) $|n| = 14$

30) $|m| = 7$

31) $|p| = 51$

32) $|x| = 50$

33) $|n| = 29$

34) $|b| = 23$

35) $|a| = 32$

36) $|p| = 48$

37) $|n| = 25$

38) $|x| = 13$

39) $|a| = 54$

40) $|p| = 6$

41) $|b| = 21$

42) $|x| = 40$

43) $|m| = 59$

44) $|a| = 43$

45) $|x| = 45$

46) $|x| = 1$

47) $|n| = 30$

48) $|x| = 3$

49) $|v| = 18$

50) $|n| = 37$

Answers to Chapter 1: Absolute Value

1) $\{7, -7\}$
2) $\{49, -49\}$
3) $\{15, -15\}$
4) $\{36, -36\}$
5) $\{41, -41\}$
6) $\{20, -20\}$
7) $\{24, -24\}$
8) $\{44, -44\}$
9) $\{12, -12\}$
10) $\{33, -33\}$
11) $\{9, -9\}$
12) $\{53, -53\}$
13) $\{47, -47\}$
14) $\{4, -4\}$
15) $\{17, -17\}$
16) $\{60, -60\}$
17) $\{39, -39\}$
18) $\{5, -5\}$
19) $\{52, -52\}$
20) $\{26, -26\}$
21) $\{31, -31\}$
22) $\{10, -10\}$
23) $\{34, -34\}$
24) $\{55, -55\}$
25) $\{22, -22\}$
26) $\{42, -42\}$
27) $\{2, -2\}$
28) $\{58, -58\}$
29) $\{14, -14\}$
30) $\{7, -7\}$
31) $\{51, -51\}$
32) $\{50, -50\}$
33) $\{29, -29\}$
34) $\{23, -23\}$
35) $\{32, -32\}$
36) $\{48, -48\}$
37) $\{25, -25\}$
38) $\{13, -13\}$
39) $\{54, -54\}$
40) $\{6, -6\}$
41) $\{21, -21\}$
42) $\{40, -40\}$
43) $\{59, -59\}$
44) $\{43, -43\}$
45) $\{45, -45\}$
46) $\{1, -1\}$
47) $\{30, -30\}$
48) $\{3, -3\}$
49) $\{18, -18\}$
50) $\{37, -37\}$

Ch.1 Questions: Adding & Subtracting Negative Numbers

Find the answer to each of the following questions.

1) $(-45) + 25 + 27 - (-43)$

2) $(-42) + (-33) - 9 - 46$

3) $(-38) + (-35) - (-10) - 34$

4) $(-35) - 7 + 15 - 21$

5) $(-32) - 50 - (-3) + (-35)$

6) $(-29) + 48 - (-22) + (-47)$

7) $(-25) + (-10) - (-41) + 42$

8) $(-22) - 32 - (-15) + 29$

9) $(-19) - 30 + (-34) - 17$

10) $(-15) - (-28) - 48 + 5$

11) $(-12) + 14 - (-28) + (-8)$

12) $(-9) + (-44) + (-46) + (-20)$

13) $(-6) + (-46) + 36 + (-32)$

14) $(-2) + (-3) + 17 - 13$

15) $1 - 39 - 43 - 0$

16) $4 - 37 + 24 - (-12)$

17) $7 + (-21) + 5 - (-24)$

18) $11 + 21 - (-13) + (-36)$

19) $14 - 20 - 12 + (-49)$

20) $17 - (-39) - (-7) + 40$

21) $20 - 3 + (-25) - 28$

22) $24 + 2 - (-44) - (-28)$

23) $30 + (-14) + (-37) + 48$

24) $27 + 44 - (-19) - (-41)$

25) $34 + (-16) + 45 + 36$

26) $37 - 26 - (-31) + 23$

27) $40 - (-32) - (-50) + 11$

28) $43 + (-34) + 33 - (-1)$

29) $50 - (-50) + 39 - (-26)$

30) $(-48) - 49 - 21 + 19$

31) $47 + 9 + 14 - (-13)$

32) $(-45) - (-9) + 2 + 7$

33) $(-41) + 33 + (-17) - (-5)$

34) $(-38) + 32 - 9 - (-18)$

35) $(-35) + (-27) - (-10) - (-30)$

36) $(-32) + 15 - (-29) - (-42)$

37) $(-28) - 14 + (-47) + 46$

38) $(-25) - (-45) - (-22) + 34$

39) $(-22) + (-2) - (-41) + (-22)$

40) $(-18) + (-4) + 42 + (-34)$

41) $(-15) - 38 + (-34) - (-47)$

42) $(-12) - (-20) + 48 - 42$

43) $(-9) - (-22) - 30 + 30$

44) $(-5) + 21 + 11 + 18$

45) $(-2) + (-38) + 36 + 5$

46) $1 + (-39) + 17 + (-7)$

47) $4 + 3 - (-1) - 38$

48) $8 - 45 - (-20) - 25$

49) $11 - 44 + 5 - 13$

50) $14 + (-15) - (-13) - 1$

Answers to Ch.1 Questions: Adding & Subtracting Negative Numbers

1) 50
2) −130
3) −97
4) −48
5) −114
6) −6
7) 48
8) −10
9) −100
10) −30
11) 22
12) −119
13) −48
14) −1
15) −81
16) 3
17) 15
18) 9
19) −67
20) 103
21) −36
22) 98
23) 27
24) 131
25) 99
26) 65
27) 133
28) 43
29) 165
30) −99
31) 83
32) −27
33) −20
34) 3
35) −22
36) 54
37) −43
38) 76
39) −5
40) −14
41) −40
42) 14
43) 13
44) 45
45) 1
46) −28
47) −30
48) −42
49) −41
50) 11

Ch.1 Questions: Multiplying & Dividing Negative Numbers

Find each product.

1) $-10 \times -9 \times -7 \times -4$

2) $-3 \times -3 \times -8 \times 3$

3) $-7 \times 8 \times -1 \times -7$

4) $0 \times -7 \times -2 \times -7$

5) $3 \times -10 \times -9 \times 3$

6) $10 \times -4 \times 4 \times -10$

7) $6 \times -1 \times -3 \times 0$

8) $-8 \times -8 \times -3 \times 0$

9) $-5 \times 3 \times -3 \times 0$

10) $-2 \times -4 \times 8 \times 3$

11) $5 \times 4 \times -4 \times 7$

12) $2 \times -6 \times 2 \times -3$

13) $6 \times 3 \times -9 \times 2$

14) $-9 \times -4 \times -5 \times -6$

15) $-6 \times 6 \times 4 \times 5$

16) $-3 \times 2 \times -6 \times -7$

17) $0 \times -1 \times 0 \times -9$

18) $4 \times -5 \times 7 \times -5$

19) $7 \times 4 \times 0 \times -10$

20) $-8 \times -3 \times -1 \times -2$

21) $10 \times 6 \times -6 \times -7$

22) $-4 \times 7 \times 5 \times 8$

23) $3 \times -2 \times -2 \times -3$

24) $2 \times -1 \times 5 \times 8$

25) $5 \times 9 \times -2 \times 5$

Find each quotient.

26) $24 \div -2$

27) $22 \div 11$

28) $36 \div 4$

29) $-64 \div 8$

30) $165 \div 11$

31) $70 \div 14$

32) $42 \div -14$

33) $120 \div -10$

34) $-63 \div -7$

35) $0 \div -4$

36) $8 \div -1$

37) $42 \div 3$

38) $30 \div 6$

39) $-27 \div 9$

40) $-156 \div 12$

41) $-135 \div -15$

42) $96 \div -12$

43) $81 \div -9$

44) $-70 \div -5$

45) $-10 \div -2$

46) $45 \div -5$

47) $-52 \div 4$

48) $72 \div 8$

49) $0 \div 11$

50) $-126 \div 14$

Answers to Ch.1 Questions: Multiplying & Dividing Negative Numbers

1) 2520	2) −216	3) −392
4) 0	5) 810	6) 1600
7) 0	8) 0	9) 0
10) 192	11) −560	12) 72
13) −324	14) 1080	15) −720
16) −252	17) 0	18) 700
19) 0	20) 48	21) 2520
22) −1120	23) −36	24) −80
25) −450	26) −12	27) 2
28) 9	29) −8	30) 15
31) 5	32) −3	33) −12
34) 9	35) 0	36) −8
37) 14	38) 5	39) −3
40) −13	41) 9	42) −8
43) −9	44) 14	45) 5
46) −9	47) −13	48) 9
49) 0	50) −9	

Chapter 1 Questions: Mixed Problems

Evaluate each expression.

1) $9 \div (3 - 6)$

2) $(-4)|2|$

3) $((-4) - 2) \times (-5)$

4) $(-6) - 4 - (-4)$

5) $4 - 6 - 3$

6) $10 \div (|5|)$

7) $9 \div ((-6) + 3)$

8) $15 \div (-3) \times (-6)$

9) $|(-5)| - 3$

10) $((-12) \div 3) - 4$

11) $(-2) + (-3) + 1$

12) $(-6)(3 + 5)$

13) $(18 - 6) \div 3$

14) $(5 - 6) \times (-5)$

15) $6 - (-3) \times (-4)$

16) $|(-6)| - 2$

17) $4 + 18 \div 3$

18) $(9 - (-3)) \div (-3)$

19) $|(-5) \times 4|$

20) $5 - 6 \times (-3)$

21) $(-2) - 12 \div (-2)$

22) $(-1)^2 + 5$

23) $|1| \times (-3)$

24) $4(3 - (-4))$

25) $((-3) - (-6))^2$

26) $(2 - 5)^2$

27) $((-4) - 3)^2$

28) $|(-5) - 5|$

29) $(-4)|6|$

30) $|(-1) \div (-1)|$

31) $4 \times 3 - 6$

32) $(-3) \times (-6) - 1$

33) $(-1) + (-4)^2$

34) $4 \div (-2)^2$

35) $3|(-6)|$

36) $5 - 3 - 5$

37) $|(-1) + 6|$

38) $(-2) + (-4) - 6$

39) $\left|1^2\right|$

40) $2 \times 5 \times (-3)$

41) $(-3) - 3^2$

42) $3 + (-6) - 5$

43) $(-4) \times (-2)^3$

44) $((-6) \times 2) \div (-6)$

45) $(1-4) \times 6$

46) $4 - \left|(-1)\right|$

47) $(-3) - \left|(-3)\right|$

48) $\left|2 - (-6)\right|$

49) $\left|2 - (-3)\right|$

50) $(5 \times 3) \div 5$

Answers to Chapter 1 Questions: Mixed Problems

1) −3
2) −8
3) 30
4) −6
5) −5
6) 2
7) −3
8) 30
9) 2
10) −8
11) −4
12) −48
13) 4
14) 5
15) −6
16) 4
17) 10
18) −4
19) 20
20) 23
21) 4
22) 6
23) −3
24) 28
25) 9
26) 9
27) 49
28) 10
29) −24
30) 1
31) 6
32) 17
33) 15
34) 1
35) 18
36) −3
37) 5
38) −12
39) 1
40) −30
41) −12
42) −8
43) 32
44) 2
45) −18
46) 3
47) −6
48) 8
49) 5
50) 3

Chapter 2 Questions: Greatest Common Factor

Find the Greatest Common Factor of each.

1) 50, 20　　　　　　　　2) 33, 44

3) 22, 33　　　　　　　　4) 23, 49

5) 36, 6　　　　　　　　 6) 33, 39

7) 35, 42　　　　　　　　8) 36, 48

9) 24, 36　　　　　　　 10) 24, 48

11) 24, 32　　　　　　　12) 12, 48

13) 36, 12　　　　　　　14) 45, 36

15) 45, 18　　　　　　　16) 27, 18

17) 30, 45　　　　　　　18) 24, 4

19) 50, 30　　　　　　　20) 34, 24

21) 30, 40　　　　　　　22) 42, 18

23) 14, 35　　　　　　　24) 14, 28

25) 36, 18　　　　　　　26) 16, 40

27) 32, 20　　　　　　　28) 20, 40

29) 13, 2　　　　　　　 30) 44, 22

31) 40, 50　　　　　　　32) 27, 36

33) 25, 50　　　　　　　34) 44, 14

35) 34, 42　　　　　　　36) 49, 14

37) 48, 30　　　　　　　38) 42, 12

39) 39, 42   40) 35, 21

41) 40, 36   42) 40, 12

43) 15, 25   44) 6, 30

45) 44, 32   46) 36, 42

47) 10, 46   48) 21, 5

49) 42, 21   50) 12, 32

Answers to Chapter 2 Questions: Greatest Common Factor

1) 10	2) 11	3) 11
4) 1	5) 6	6) 3
7) 7	8) 12	9) 12
10) 24	11) 8	12) 12
13) 12	14) 9	15) 9
16) 9	17) 15	18) 4
19) 10	20) 2	21) 10
22) 6	23) 7	24) 14
25) 18	26) 8	27) 4
28) 20	29) 1	30) 22
31) 10	32) 9	33) 25
34) 2	35) 2	36) 7
37) 6	38) 6	39) 3
40) 7	41) 4	42) 4
43) 5	44) 6	45) 4
46) 6	47) 2	48) 1
49) 21	50) 4	

Chapter 2 Questions: Lowest Common Multiple

Find the Lowest Common Multiple of each.

1) 20, 30   2) 24, 30

3) 24, 16   4) 24, 14

5) 30, 4   6) 28, 21

7) 40, 32   8) 39, 30

9) 36, 30   10) 10, 18

11) 40, 24   12) 35, 21

13) 18, 24   14) 16, 10

15) 34, 4   16) 15, 25

17) 35, 14   18) 8, 28

19) 35, 25   20) 18, 27

21) 33, 4   22) 12, 32

23) 27, 24   24) 10, 40

25) 26, 40   26) 18, 39

27) 15, 20   28) 12, 18

29) 15, 35   30) 28, 32

31) 40, 30   32) 35, 2

33) 32, 24   34) 12, 20

35) 27, 30   36) 21, 14

37) 8, 22   38) 40, 25

39) 35, 28

40) 12, 30

41) 33, 18

42) 36, 27

43) 16, 28

44) 8, 18

45) 15, 27

46) 18, 30

47) 40, 16

48) 15, 40

49) 33, 36

50) 28, 40

Answers to Chapter 2 Questions: Lowest Common Multiple

1) 60	2) 120	3) 48
4) 168	5) 60	6) 84
7) 160	8) 390	9) 180
10) 90	11) 120	12) 105
13) 72	14) 80	15) 68
16) 75	17) 70	18) 56
19) 175	20) 54	21) 132
22) 96	23) 216	24) 40
25) 520	26) 234	27) 60
28) 36	29) 105	30) 224
31) 120	32) 70	33) 96
34) 60	35) 270	36) 42
37) 88	38) 200	39) 140
40) 60	41) 198	42) 108
43) 112	44) 72	45) 135
46) 90	47) 80	48) 120
49) 396	50) 280	

Chapter 2 Questions: Fractions in The Simplest Form

Write each of the following fractions in its simplest form.

1) $\dfrac{8}{12}$

2) $\dfrac{54}{66}$

3) $\dfrac{60}{144}$

4) $\dfrac{18}{42}$

5) $\dfrac{12}{30}$

6) $\dfrac{42}{66}$

7) $\dfrac{18}{126}$

8) $\dfrac{20}{40}$

9) $\dfrac{24}{36}$

10) $\dfrac{54}{99}$

11) $\dfrac{18}{81}$

12) $\dfrac{6}{12}$

13) $\dfrac{20}{36}$

14) $\dfrac{27}{99}$

15) $\dfrac{12}{18}$

16) $\dfrac{36}{63}$

17) $\dfrac{16}{20}$

18) $\dfrac{12}{120}$

19) $\dfrac{12}{36}$

20) $\dfrac{84}{96}$

21) $\dfrac{81}{99}$

22) $\dfrac{6}{36}$

23) $\dfrac{72}{81}$

24) $\dfrac{66}{72}$

25) $\dfrac{63}{72}$

26) $\dfrac{28}{32}$

27) $\dfrac{27}{45}$

28) $\dfrac{12}{48}$

29) $\dfrac{72}{126}$

30) $\dfrac{160}{180}$

31) $\dfrac{16}{44}$

32) $\dfrac{9}{27}$

33) $\dfrac{50}{80}$

34) $\dfrac{12}{16}$

35) $\dfrac{45}{108}$

36) $\dfrac{18}{48}$

37) $\dfrac{24}{44}$

38) $\dfrac{16}{40}$

39) $\dfrac{18}{36}$

40) $\dfrac{9}{45}$

41) $\dfrac{30}{72}$

42) $\dfrac{40}{72}$

43) $\dfrac{18}{24}$

44) $\dfrac{12}{44}$

45) $\dfrac{30}{36}$

46) $\dfrac{24}{30}$

47) $\dfrac{45}{54}$

48) $\dfrac{8}{80}$

49) $\dfrac{60}{66}$

50) $\dfrac{45}{81}$

Answers to Chapter 2 Questions: Fractions in The Simplest Form

1) $\dfrac{2}{3}$ 2) $\dfrac{9}{11}$ 3) $\dfrac{5}{12}$

4) $\dfrac{3}{7}$ 5) $\dfrac{2}{5}$ 6) $\dfrac{7}{11}$

7) $\dfrac{1}{7}$ 8) $\dfrac{1}{2}$ 9) $\dfrac{2}{3}$

10) $\dfrac{6}{11}$ 11) $\dfrac{2}{9}$ 12) $\dfrac{1}{2}$

13) $\dfrac{5}{9}$ 14) $\dfrac{3}{11}$ 15) $\dfrac{2}{3}$

16) $\dfrac{4}{7}$ 17) $\dfrac{4}{5}$ 18) $\dfrac{1}{10}$

19) $\dfrac{1}{3}$ 20) $\dfrac{7}{8}$ 21) $\dfrac{9}{11}$

22) $\dfrac{1}{6}$ 23) $\dfrac{8}{9}$ 24) $\dfrac{11}{12}$

25) $\dfrac{7}{8}$ 26) $\dfrac{7}{8}$ 27) $\dfrac{3}{5}$

28) $\dfrac{1}{4}$ 29) $\dfrac{4}{7}$ 30) $\dfrac{8}{9}$

31) $\dfrac{4}{11}$ 32) $\dfrac{1}{3}$ 33) $\dfrac{5}{8}$

34) $\dfrac{3}{4}$ 35) $\dfrac{5}{12}$ 36) $\dfrac{3}{8}$

37) $\dfrac{6}{11}$ 38) $\dfrac{2}{5}$ 39) $\dfrac{1}{2}$

40) $\dfrac{1}{5}$ 41) $\dfrac{5}{12}$ 42) $\dfrac{5}{9}$

43) $\dfrac{3}{4}$ 44) $\dfrac{3}{11}$ 45) $\dfrac{5}{6}$

46) $\dfrac{4}{5}$ 47) $\dfrac{5}{6}$ 48) $\dfrac{1}{10}$

49) $\frac{10}{11}$

50) $\frac{5}{9}$

Ch.2 Questions: Changing Fractions to Mixed Numbers

Write each of the following fractions as a mixed number. Remember to write the final answer in the simplest form.

1) $\dfrac{32}{12}$

2) $\dfrac{18}{12}$

3) $\dfrac{24}{18}$

4) $\dfrac{20}{8}$

5) $\dfrac{160}{100}$

6) $\dfrac{54}{36}$

7) $\dfrac{144}{54}$

8) $\dfrac{28}{16}$

9) $\dfrac{56}{24}$

10) $\dfrac{40}{24}$

11) $\dfrac{72}{54}$

12) $\dfrac{63}{45}$

13) $\dfrac{36}{27}$

14) $\dfrac{12}{8}$

15) $\dfrac{28}{24}$

16) $\dfrac{140}{80}$

17) $\dfrac{126}{108}$

18) $\dfrac{20}{16}$

19) $\dfrac{96}{60}$ 20) $\dfrac{90}{72}$

21) $\dfrac{28}{20}$ 22) $\dfrac{42}{36}$

23) $\dfrac{36}{24}$ 24) $\dfrac{120}{100}$

25) $\dfrac{54}{45}$ 26) $\dfrac{42}{12}$

27) $\dfrac{160}{60}$ 28) $\dfrac{30}{12}$

29) $\dfrac{63}{27}$ 30) $\dfrac{56}{40}$

31) $\dfrac{70}{40}$ 32) $\dfrac{126}{90}$

33) $\dfrac{42}{30}$ 34) $\dfrac{60}{50}$

35) $\dfrac{16}{12}$ 36) $\dfrac{40}{32}$

37) $\dfrac{32}{28}$ 38) $\dfrac{63}{18}$

39) $\dfrac{126}{54}$

40) $\dfrac{45}{27}$

41) $\dfrac{84}{36}$

42) $\dfrac{63}{36}$

43) $\dfrac{48}{36}$

44) $\dfrac{30}{24}$

45) $\dfrac{126}{72}$

46) $\dfrac{28}{12}$

47) $\dfrac{72}{45}$

48) $\dfrac{48}{18}$

49) $\dfrac{27}{18}$

50) $\dfrac{100}{60}$

Answers to Ch.2 Questions: Changing Fractions to Mixed Numbers

1) $2\frac{2}{3}$
2) $1\frac{1}{2}$
3) $1\frac{1}{3}$
4) $2\frac{1}{2}$
5) $1\frac{3}{5}$
6) $1\frac{1}{2}$
7) $2\frac{2}{3}$
8) $1\frac{3}{4}$
9) $2\frac{1}{3}$
10) $1\frac{2}{3}$
11) $1\frac{1}{3}$
12) $1\frac{2}{5}$
13) $1\frac{1}{3}$
14) $1\frac{1}{2}$
15) $1\frac{1}{6}$
16) $1\frac{3}{4}$
17) $1\frac{1}{6}$
18) $1\frac{1}{4}$
19) $1\frac{3}{5}$
20) $1\frac{1}{4}$
21) $1\frac{2}{5}$
22) $1\frac{1}{6}$
23) $1\frac{1}{2}$
24) $1\frac{1}{5}$
25) $1\frac{1}{5}$
26) $3\frac{1}{2}$
27) $2\frac{2}{3}$
28) $2\frac{1}{2}$
29) $2\frac{1}{3}$
30) $1\frac{2}{5}$
31) $1\frac{3}{4}$
32) $1\frac{2}{5}$
33) $1\frac{2}{5}$
34) $1\frac{1}{5}$
35) $1\frac{1}{3}$
36) $1\frac{1}{4}$
37) $1\frac{1}{7}$
38) $3\frac{1}{2}$
39) $2\frac{1}{3}$
40) $1\frac{2}{3}$
41) $2\frac{1}{3}$
42) $1\frac{3}{4}$
43) $1\frac{1}{3}$
44) $1\frac{1}{4}$
45) $1\frac{3}{4}$
46) $2\frac{1}{3}$
47) $1\frac{3}{5}$
48) $2\frac{2}{3}$

49) $1\frac{1}{2}$ 50) $1\frac{2}{3}$

Chapter 2 Questions: Changing Fractions to Decimals

Write each as a decimal. Round to the hundredths place.

1) $7\dfrac{1}{25}$

2) $2\dfrac{33}{100}$

3) $6\dfrac{47}{70}$

4) $4\dfrac{1}{2}$

5) $3\dfrac{9}{20}$

6) $8\dfrac{87}{100}$

7) $\dfrac{91}{100}$

8) $\dfrac{3}{50}$

9) $\dfrac{1}{8}$

10) $\dfrac{11}{16}$

11) $\dfrac{2}{25}$

12) $\dfrac{1}{5}$

13) $\dfrac{5}{8}$

14) $\dfrac{4}{5}$

15) $\dfrac{1}{4}$

16) $\dfrac{1}{10}$

17) $\dfrac{3}{4}$

18) $\dfrac{79}{100}$

19) $\dfrac{1}{2}$

20) $\dfrac{3}{10}$

21) $\dfrac{4}{75}$

22) $\dfrac{31}{39}$

23) $\dfrac{7}{10}$

24) $\dfrac{93}{100}$

25) $\dfrac{8}{15}$

26) $2\dfrac{11}{16}$

27) $5\dfrac{1}{5}$

28) $8\dfrac{3}{4}$

29) $3\dfrac{7}{44}$

30) $6\dfrac{89}{95}$

31) $4\dfrac{4}{5}$

32) $\dfrac{29}{38}$

33) $\dfrac{11}{25}$

34) $\dfrac{87}{100}$

35) $\dfrac{13}{15}$

36) $\dfrac{29}{100}$

37) $\dfrac{9}{10}$

38) $\dfrac{64}{75}$

39) $\dfrac{44}{45}$

40) $\dfrac{3}{5}$

41) $\dfrac{2}{5}$

42) $\dfrac{1}{3}$

43) $4\dfrac{99}{100}$

44) $7\dfrac{21}{73}$

45) $2\dfrac{9}{10}$

46) $9\dfrac{33}{50}$

47) $8\dfrac{3}{10}$

48) $4\dfrac{59}{60}$

49) $\dfrac{38}{75}$

50) $\dfrac{14}{25}$

Answers to Chapter 2 Questions: Changing Fractions to Decimals

1) 7.04
2) 2.33
3) 6.67
4) 4.5
5) 3.45
6) 8.87
7) 0.91
8) 0.06
9) 0.13
10) 0.69
11) 0.08
12) 0.2
13) 0.63
14) 0.8
15) 0.25
16) 0.1
17) 0.75
18) 0.79
19) 0.5
20) 0.3
21) 0.05
22) 0.79
23) 0.7
24) 0.93
25) 0.53
26) 2.69
27) 5.2
28) 8.75
29) 3.16
30) 6.94
31) 4.8
32) 0.76
33) 0.44
34) 0.87
35) 0.87
36) 0.29
37) 0.9
38) 0.85
39) 0.98
40) 0.6
41) 0.4
42) 0.33
43) 4.99
44) 7.29
45) 2.9
46) 9.66
47) 8.3
48) 4.98
49) 0.51
50) 0.56

Ch.2 Questions: Adding & Subtracting Fractions

Evaluate each expression. Write your answer as a mixed number when possible.

1) $3\frac{1}{5} + 1\frac{5}{8}$

2) $1\frac{2}{5} + \frac{5}{3}$

3) $1\frac{1}{4} + 4\frac{3}{4}$

4) $3\frac{1}{3} + 1\frac{1}{2}$

5) $2\frac{3}{4} + 4\frac{4}{5}$

6) $4\frac{2}{3} + \frac{2}{5}$

7) $\frac{1}{2} - \frac{1}{6}$

8) $\frac{1}{2} + 2\frac{2}{5}$

9) $4\frac{3}{5} + 2\frac{2}{3}$

10) $\frac{1}{2} + \frac{2}{3}$

11) $\frac{1}{3} + 1\frac{1}{2}$

12) $5 - \frac{5}{3}$

13) $4\frac{1}{6} - \frac{1}{3}$

14) $4\frac{1}{2} - 1\frac{5}{7}$

15) $\frac{10}{7} + \frac{1}{4}$

16) $1 + \frac{8}{7}$

17) $4\frac{6}{7} - \frac{3}{7}$

18) $8 - 2\frac{1}{4}$

19) $\dfrac{6}{5} + \dfrac{5}{8}$

20) $\dfrac{1}{5} + \dfrac{8}{5}$

21) $2 - \dfrac{4}{3}$

22) $2 - \dfrac{11}{6}$

23) $8 + \dfrac{3}{4}$

24) $\dfrac{4}{3} - \dfrac{1}{6}$

25) $1\dfrac{1}{2} + \dfrac{5}{7}$

26) $\dfrac{5}{3} + \dfrac{2}{3}$

27) $2\dfrac{1}{2} - \dfrac{1}{2}$

28) $1\dfrac{5}{8} - \dfrac{3}{5}$

29) $1\dfrac{1}{8} + \dfrac{1}{2}$

30) $5\dfrac{1}{3} + \dfrac{1}{2}$

31) $3\dfrac{1}{8} - \dfrac{1}{4}$

32) $3\dfrac{5}{7} + 2\dfrac{5}{7}$

33) $\dfrac{6}{7} - \dfrac{2}{5}$

34) $3\dfrac{1}{6} - \dfrac{3}{2}$

35) $3\dfrac{3}{7} + \dfrac{5}{8}$

36) $2\dfrac{3}{5} - 2\dfrac{3}{5}$

37) $4\dfrac{5}{6} - 3\dfrac{1}{6}$

38) $\dfrac{15}{8} - \dfrac{5}{7}$

39) $3\frac{1}{5} - \frac{9}{8}$

40) $4\frac{1}{4} + \frac{5}{3}$

41) $2\frac{1}{4} + 7\frac{1}{2}$

42) $2\frac{7}{8} - \frac{2}{5}$

43) $\frac{2}{7} + 4\frac{1}{7}$

44) $1 + 4\frac{1}{4}$

45) $6 - 3\frac{1}{7}$

46) $\frac{3}{2} - \frac{4}{3}$

47) $1 + 4\frac{1}{2}$

48) $1 + \frac{3}{4}$

49) $2 + 2\frac{1}{5}$

50) $4\frac{3}{4} + \frac{5}{7}$

Answers to Ch.2 Questions: Adding & Subtracting Fractions

1) $4\dfrac{33}{40}$
2) $3\dfrac{1}{15}$
3) 6
4) $4\dfrac{5}{6}$
5) $7\dfrac{11}{20}$
6) $5\dfrac{1}{15}$
7) $\dfrac{1}{3}$
8) $2\dfrac{9}{10}$
9) $7\dfrac{4}{15}$
10) $1\dfrac{1}{6}$
11) $1\dfrac{5}{6}$
12) $3\dfrac{1}{3}$
13) $3\dfrac{5}{6}$
14) $2\dfrac{11}{14}$
15) $1\dfrac{19}{28}$
16) $2\dfrac{1}{7}$
17) $4\dfrac{3}{7}$
18) $5\dfrac{3}{4}$
19) $1\dfrac{33}{40}$
20) $1\dfrac{4}{5}$
21) $\dfrac{2}{3}$
22) $\dfrac{1}{6}$
23) $8\dfrac{3}{4}$
24) $1\dfrac{1}{6}$
25) $2\dfrac{3}{14}$
26) $2\dfrac{1}{3}$
27) 2
28) $1\dfrac{1}{40}$
29) $1\dfrac{5}{8}$
30) $5\dfrac{5}{6}$
31) $2\dfrac{7}{8}$
32) $6\dfrac{3}{7}$
33) $\dfrac{16}{35}$
34) $1\dfrac{2}{3}$
35) $4\dfrac{3}{56}$
36) 0
37) $1\dfrac{2}{3}$
38) $1\dfrac{9}{56}$
39) $2\dfrac{3}{40}$
40) $5\dfrac{11}{12}$
41) $9\dfrac{3}{4}$
42) $2\dfrac{19}{40}$
43) $4\dfrac{3}{7}$
44) $5\dfrac{1}{4}$
45) $2\dfrac{6}{7}$
46) $\dfrac{1}{6}$
47) $5\dfrac{1}{2}$
48) $1\dfrac{3}{4}$

49) $4\dfrac{1}{5}$

50) $5\dfrac{13}{28}$

Chapter 2 Questions: Multiplying Fractions

Find each product. Write your answer as a mixed number when possible.

1) $5\dfrac{5}{6} \times -\dfrac{3}{2}$

2) $4\dfrac{6}{7} \times -\dfrac{1}{2}$

3) $-\dfrac{1}{3} \times -\dfrac{2}{3}$

4) $\dfrac{3}{2} \times -\dfrac{1}{2}$

5) $-2\dfrac{9}{10} \times \dfrac{17}{10}$

6) $-2\dfrac{1}{2} \times 3$

7) $-\dfrac{1}{3} \times \dfrac{5}{7}$

8) $1\dfrac{1}{3} \times -2$

9) $5\dfrac{5}{8} \times -2\dfrac{4}{5}$

10) $-3\dfrac{1}{2} \times -1\dfrac{4}{5}$

11) $-3\dfrac{1}{3} \times 4\dfrac{5}{9}$

12) $-\dfrac{9}{5} \times \dfrac{1}{2}$

13) $3\dfrac{3}{7} \times -\dfrac{4}{3}$

14) $-3\dfrac{2}{5} \times 4\dfrac{1}{3}$

15) $1\dfrac{1}{7} \times -\dfrac{2}{3}$

16) $-2\dfrac{7}{8} \times \dfrac{3}{2}$

17) $1\dfrac{4}{9} \times -3\dfrac{5}{6}$

18) $-3\dfrac{3}{7} \times \dfrac{3}{4}$

19) $-2\dfrac{1}{6} \times \dfrac{1}{2}$

20) $-2\dfrac{6}{7} \times \dfrac{5}{6}$

21) $-2\dfrac{9}{10} \times -\dfrac{8}{5}$

22) $5\dfrac{4}{9} \times -2$

23) $\dfrac{11}{10} \times -\dfrac{11}{9}$

24) $3\dfrac{1}{5} \times -\dfrac{1}{2}$

25) $-1\dfrac{1}{2} \times \dfrac{1}{7}$

26) $-3\dfrac{1}{4} \times -2$

27) $-\dfrac{5}{4} \times -\dfrac{6}{5}$

28) $-9 \times \dfrac{1}{2}$

29) $-\dfrac{4}{3} \times \dfrac{1}{10}$

30) $-\dfrac{11}{9} \times -\dfrac{1}{4}$

31) $-8\dfrac{9}{10} \times \dfrac{1}{6}$

32) $-9 \times -\dfrac{3}{2}$

33) $5\dfrac{3}{4} \times -1\dfrac{3}{4}$

34) $-2 \times \dfrac{11}{6}$

35) $2 \times -\dfrac{2}{5}$

36) $-1\dfrac{4}{9} \times -10$

37) $4\dfrac{7}{10} \times -\dfrac{17}{10}$

38) $-5 \times -\dfrac{5}{8}$

39) $1\dfrac{1}{8} \times -2\dfrac{1}{2}$

40) $-3\dfrac{1}{9} \times -\dfrac{1}{9}$

41) $\dfrac{6}{5} \times -\dfrac{4}{3}$

42) $4\dfrac{1}{2} \times -2\dfrac{1}{10}$

43) $-3\dfrac{3}{8} \times \dfrac{1}{3}$

44) $3\dfrac{2}{9} \times -\dfrac{11}{9}$

45) $2\dfrac{3}{4} \times -6$

46) $-1\dfrac{8}{9} \times \dfrac{3}{5}$

47) $-2\dfrac{4}{7} \times -\dfrac{11}{6}$

48) $2\dfrac{5}{7} \times -1\dfrac{2}{9}$

49) $-\dfrac{5}{3} \times \dfrac{17}{10}$

50) $5\dfrac{4}{7} \times -1\dfrac{4}{7}$

Answers to Chapter 2 Questions: Multiplying Fractions

1) $-8\dfrac{3}{4}$
2) $-2\dfrac{3}{7}$
3) $\dfrac{2}{9}$
4) $-\dfrac{3}{4}$
5) $-4\dfrac{93}{100}$
6) $-7\dfrac{1}{2}$
7) $-\dfrac{5}{21}$
8) $-2\dfrac{2}{3}$
9) $-15\dfrac{3}{4}$
10) $6\dfrac{3}{10}$
11) $-15\dfrac{5}{27}$
12) $-\dfrac{9}{10}$
13) $-4\dfrac{4}{7}$
14) $-14\dfrac{11}{15}$
15) $-\dfrac{16}{21}$
16) $-4\dfrac{5}{16}$
17) $-5\dfrac{29}{54}$
18) $-2\dfrac{4}{7}$
19) $-1\dfrac{1}{12}$
20) $-2\dfrac{8}{21}$
21) $4\dfrac{16}{25}$
22) $-10\dfrac{8}{9}$
23) $-1\dfrac{31}{90}$
24) $-1\dfrac{3}{5}$
25) $-\dfrac{3}{14}$
26) $6\dfrac{1}{2}$
27) $1\dfrac{1}{2}$
28) $-4\dfrac{1}{2}$
29) $-\dfrac{2}{15}$
30) $\dfrac{11}{36}$
31) $-1\dfrac{29}{60}$
32) $13\dfrac{1}{2}$
33) $-10\dfrac{1}{16}$
34) $-3\dfrac{2}{3}$
35) $-\dfrac{4}{5}$
36) $14\dfrac{4}{9}$
37) $-7\dfrac{99}{100}$
38) $3\dfrac{1}{8}$
39) $-2\dfrac{13}{16}$
40) $\dfrac{28}{81}$
41) $-1\dfrac{3}{5}$
42) $-9\dfrac{9}{20}$
43) $-1\dfrac{1}{8}$
44) $-3\dfrac{76}{81}$
45) $-16\dfrac{1}{2}$
46) $-1\dfrac{2}{15}$
47) $4\dfrac{5}{7}$
48) $-3\dfrac{20}{63}$

49) $-2\dfrac{5}{6}$

50) $-8\dfrac{37}{49}$

Chapter 2 Questions: Dividing Fractions

Find each quotient. Write your answer as a mixed number when possible.

1) $-1\dfrac{5}{9} \div 4\dfrac{1}{6}$

2) $\dfrac{1}{3} \div -1\dfrac{5}{6}$

3) $1 \div -2\dfrac{4}{5}$

4) $\dfrac{-9}{5} \div 1\dfrac{3}{5}$

5) $\dfrac{1}{10} \div \dfrac{-1}{6}$

6) $\dfrac{-8}{9} \div \dfrac{3}{5}$

7) $\dfrac{-3}{2} \div -3$

8) $\dfrac{-11}{7} \div \dfrac{-4}{5}$

9) $\dfrac{-8}{5} \div \dfrac{-5}{4}$

10) $-2 \div \dfrac{-2}{3}$

11) $1 \div \dfrac{3}{4}$

12) $-2\dfrac{3}{7} \div \dfrac{-4}{3}$

13) $-1\dfrac{8}{9} \div \dfrac{4}{3}$

14) $\dfrac{-5}{3} \div \dfrac{3}{2}$

15) $-2\dfrac{2}{5} \div \dfrac{-1}{2}$

16) $4\dfrac{1}{3} \div -1$

17) $-7\dfrac{1}{2} \div -2$

18) $\dfrac{-3}{2} \div \dfrac{3}{2}$

19) $\dfrac{-11}{8} \div \dfrac{-7}{5}$

20) $\dfrac{5}{4} \div 2\dfrac{9}{10}$

21) $3\dfrac{5}{9} \div 4\dfrac{4}{9}$

22) $\dfrac{1}{10} \div -2\dfrac{2}{9}$

23) $3\dfrac{5}{6} \div -3$

24) $\dfrac{-10}{9} \div 4\dfrac{2}{9}$

25) $\dfrac{-1}{2} \div \dfrac{3}{8}$

26) $\dfrac{4}{3} \div -2\dfrac{5}{8}$

27) $\dfrac{-5}{7} \div -3\dfrac{1}{7}$

28) $\dfrac{8}{9} \div -1\dfrac{5}{8}$

29) $\dfrac{-2}{5} \div -8$

30) $-1 \div \dfrac{5}{8}$

31) $-2 \div -3\dfrac{1}{7}$

32) $1\dfrac{3}{4} \div \dfrac{1}{6}$

33) $-1\dfrac{6}{7} \div 5\dfrac{3}{5}$

34) $4\dfrac{3}{10} \div 3\dfrac{1}{6}$

35) $4\dfrac{1}{4} \div -1\dfrac{5}{6}$

36) $-3\dfrac{9}{10} : \dfrac{-2}{5}$

37) $-4 \div \dfrac{6}{5}$

38) $1\dfrac{1}{8} \div \dfrac{9}{5}$

39) $-1 \div \dfrac{-5}{4}$

40) $\dfrac{4}{5} \div \dfrac{6}{5}$

41) $-2\dfrac{1}{3} \div \dfrac{3}{4}$

42) $\dfrac{-17}{10} \div \dfrac{1}{2}$

43) $0 \div \dfrac{-1}{3}$

44) $\dfrac{1}{7} \div \dfrac{4}{3}$

45) $3\dfrac{1}{6} \div 2$

46) $2\dfrac{3}{4} \div -1$

47) $\dfrac{-1}{3} \div \dfrac{1}{2}$

48) $\dfrac{7}{10} \div \dfrac{-1}{2}$

49) $-1\dfrac{7}{10} \div -2$

50) $-3\dfrac{3}{8} \div \dfrac{-7}{10}$

Answers to Chapter 2 Questions: Dividing Fractions

1) $-\dfrac{28}{75}$
2) $-\dfrac{2}{11}$
3) $-\dfrac{5}{14}$
4) $-1\dfrac{1}{8}$
5) $-\dfrac{3}{5}$
6) $-1\dfrac{13}{27}$
7) $\dfrac{1}{2}$
8) $1\dfrac{27}{28}$
9) $1\dfrac{7}{25}$
10) 3
11) $1\dfrac{1}{3}$
12) $1\dfrac{23}{28}$
13) $-1\dfrac{5}{12}$
14) $-1\dfrac{1}{9}$
15) $4\dfrac{4}{5}$
16) $-4\dfrac{1}{3}$
17) $3\dfrac{3}{4}$
18) -1
19) $\dfrac{55}{56}$
20) $\dfrac{25}{58}$
21) $\dfrac{4}{5}$
22) $-\dfrac{9}{200}$
23) $-1\dfrac{5}{18}$
24) $-\dfrac{5}{19}$
25) $-1\dfrac{1}{3}$
26) $-\dfrac{32}{63}$
27) $\dfrac{5}{22}$
28) $-\dfrac{64}{117}$
29) $\dfrac{1}{20}$
30) $-1\dfrac{3}{5}$
31) $\dfrac{7}{11}$
32) $10\dfrac{1}{2}$
33) $-\dfrac{65}{196}$
34) $1\dfrac{34}{95}$
35) $-2\dfrac{7}{22}$
36) $9\dfrac{3}{4}$
37) $-3\dfrac{1}{3}$
38) $\dfrac{5}{8}$
39) $\dfrac{4}{5}$
40) $\dfrac{2}{3}$
41) $-3\dfrac{1}{9}$
42) $-3\dfrac{2}{5}$
43) 0
44) $\dfrac{3}{28}$
45) $1\dfrac{7}{12}$
46) $-2\dfrac{3}{4}$
47) $-\dfrac{2}{3}$
48) $-1\dfrac{2}{5}$

49) $\dfrac{17}{20}$

50) $4\dfrac{23}{28}$

Math Practice by Kareem Gouda www.SKOOLOO.com

Chapter 3 Questions: Decimal Place Values

Write the name of each decimal place indicated.

1) 1.7817<u>8</u>7

2) 7.<u>5</u>3

3) 9.920<u>5</u>2

4) 9.1611<u>4</u>66

5) 1.40108<u>4</u>6

6) 1.64<u>0</u>63

7) 3.8<u>8</u>145

8) 1.0<u>2</u>2

9) 1.2619<u>0</u>4

10) 2.402<u>5</u>50

11) 4.643<u>4</u>98

12) 9.882<u>0</u>48

13) 8.0<u>2</u>286

14) 3.26350<u>7</u>2

15) 3.4<u>0</u>23

16) 0.74396<u>5</u>2

17) 5.9848<u>0</u>50

18) 1.123<u>4</u>4

19) 1.<u>3</u>6

20) 3.5<u>0</u>5

21) 5.7<u>4</u>375

22) 6.984<u>3</u>99

23) 5.13521<u>9</u>8

24) 7.37485<u>7</u>7

25) 6.51<u>5</u>6

26) 1.<u>8</u>5

27) 8.<u>0</u>951

28) 1.2<u>3</u>6

29) 9.4766<u>2</u>45

30) 2.6152<u>6</u>2

31) 7.<u>8</u>56

32) 3.09<u>7</u>73

33) 2.<u>2</u>3

34) 8.47<u>7</u>110

35) 8.618<u>9</u>3

36) 1.859679<u>3</u>

37) 7.1974<u>2</u>73

38) 7.3<u>3</u>80

39) 8.5_79

40) 7.71852_51

41) 1.959_343

42) 5.190_083

43) 7.33983_11

44) 2.570_45

45) 9.720_399

46) 3.9_699

47) 1.1007_589

48) 3.4414_98

49) 8.6802_489

50) 7.82_1886

Answers to Chapter 3 Questions: Decimal Place Values

1) hundred-thousandths
2) tenths
3) ten-thousandths
4) hundred-thousandths
5) millionths
6) thousandths
7) hundredths
8) hundredths
9) millionths
10) ten-thousandths
11) hundred-thousandths
12) hundred-thousandths
13) hundredths
14) millionths
15) thousandths
16) millionths
17) hundred-thousandths
18) ten-thousandths
19) tenths
20) hundredths
21) hundredths
22) ten-thousandths
23) millionths
24) millionths
25) thousandths
26) tenths
27) tenths
28) hundredths
29) hundred-thousandths
30) hundred-thousandths
31) tenths
32) thousandths
33) tenths
34) thousandths
35) ten-thousandths
36) millionths
37) hundred-thousandths
38) hundredths
39) hundredths
40) millionths
41) ten-thousandths
42) ten-thousandths
43) millionths
44) ten-thousandths
45) ten-thousandths
46) hundredths
47) hundred-thousandths
48) hundred-thousandths
49) millionths
50) thousandths

Chapter 3 Questions: Rounding Decimal Numbers

Round each number to the place indicated.

1) 1.062706

2) 7.2013447

3) 5.94

4) 8.6828027

5) 2.8216427

6) 3.062290

7) 6.20311

8) 6.542759

9) 8.78359

10) 7.924

11) 1.162057

12) 2.3036

13) 5.5445953

14) 6.7831633

15) 9.92490

16) 8.1756233

17) 6.3144611

18) 3.55501

19) 1.89593

20) 8.034570

21) 0.2753981

22) 1.41603

23) 5.6578769

24) 8.8964269

25) 0.0373499

26) 6.278984

27) 1.41672

28) 4.8982

29) 3.657942

30) 6.137831

31) 7.3786797

32) 2.5193997

33) 3.75

34) 4.99997

35) 5.139697

36) 7.37

37) 9.599

38) 2.7609035

39) 5.9095_4_3

40) 7.2_4_03

41) 6.48_1_00

42) 0.62_0_85

43) 4.8604_9_0

44) 6.0013_1_81

45) 5.2409_5_81

46) 8.4817_9_6

47) 3.622_4_16

48) 9.8_6_12

49) 2.0_0_280

50) 4._2_437

Answers to Chapter 3 Questions: Rounding Decimal Numbers

1) 1.0627
2) 7.201345
3) 5.9
4) 8.68280
5) 2.821643
6) 3.06229
7) 6.203
8) 6.543
9) 8.7836
10) 7.9
11) 1.1621
12) 2.3
13) 5.54460
14) 6.783163
15) 9.92
16) 8.175623
17) 6.31446
18) 3.555
19) 1.90
20) 8.0346
21) 0.27540
22) 1.42
23) 5.657877
24) 8.896427
25) 0.037350
26) 6.27898
27) 1.4167
28) 4.9
29) 3.6579
30) 6.1378
31) 7.378680
32) 2.519400
33) 3.8
34) 5.000
35) 5.1397
36) 7.4
37) 9.60
38) 2.760904
39) 5.90954
40) 7.24
41) 6.481
42) 0.621
43) 4.86049
44) 6.00132
45) 5.24096
46) 8.48180
47) 3.6224
48) 9.86
49) 2.00
50) 4.2

Ch.3 Questions: Adding & Subtracting Decimal Numbers

Evaluate each expression.

1) 12 + 15.5

2) 15.9 + 0.5

3) 8.2 + 6.8

4) 11.9 – 5.8

5) 4.2 + 12.1

6) 8.1 + 4.7

7) 7.9 + 11.1

8) 7.5 + 5.1

9) 4 + 0.3

10) 4.6 + 2.1

11) 5.6 + 11.5

12) 10.4 + 7.8

13) 9 + 14.7

14) 7.98 – 1.5

15) 9.065 + 2.5

16) 12.1 – 2.3

17) 8.2 + 1.3

18) 4.4 + 8.7

19) 16 + 3.15

20) 13 + 9.8

21) 15.96 – 12.4

22) 4.2 + 12.9

23) 0.3 + 11.9

24) 12.5 – 10.8

25) 7.6 + 15.22

26) 12.4 – 1.1

27) 8.7 + 5.7

28) 3.7 + 15.2

29) 8.4 – 6.4

30) 4.6 – 1.17

31) 8.3 + 4.2

32) 4.5 – 3.1

33) 9.6 + 2.4

34) 4.3 + 9.5

35) 0.5 + 8.4

36) 7 + 11.8

37) 7.29 + 8.86

38) 12.6 + 13.7

39) 8.7 + 12.7

40) 6.3 + 7.4

41) 8.6 − 2.9

42) 15.879 − 11.4

43) 9.75 − 3.9

44) 8.1 + 12.3

45) 5.2 − 1.7

46) 2.3 + 14.8

47) 15.5 − 11.8

48) 12.9 + 12.4

49) 13.7 − 13.3

50) 12.8 + 10.3

Answers to Ch.3 Questions: Adding & Subtracting Decimal Numbers

1) 27.5	2) 16.4	3) 15
4) 6.1	5) 16.3	6) 12.8
7) 19	8) 12.6	9) 4.3
10) 6.7	11) 17.1	12) 18.2
13) 23.7	14) 6.48	15) 11.565
16) 9.8	17) 9.5	18) 13.1
19) 19.15	20) 22.8	21) 3.56
22) 17.1	23) 12.2	24) 1.7
25) 22.82	26) 11.3	27) 14.4
28) 18.9	29) 2	30) 3.43
31) 12.5	32) 1.4	33) 12
34) 13.8	35) 8.9	36) 18.8
37) 16.15	38) 26.3	39) 21.4
40) 13.7	41) 5.7	42) 4.479
43) 5.85	44) 20.4	45) 3.5
46) 17.1	47) 3.7	48) 25.3
49) 0.4	50) 23.1	

Chapter 3 Questions: Multiplying Decimal Numbers

Find each product.

1) -4.7×-3.3

2) -9.2×1.6

3) -0.2×-4.6

4) -6.41×-6.4

5) -1.2×3.7

6) 7.8×-2.5

7) -2.7×-7.131

8) 6.8×-9.583

9) -4.2×-0.4

10) 5.3×-6.6

11) -5.3×7.4

12) -1.3×-1.7

13) -6.8×-4.5

14) 0.2×-3.7

15) -8.3×3.3

16) 1.2×-2.9

17) -9.3×-8.6

18) 1.2×-6.2

19) -0.3×2.57

20) -1.3×-6.5

21) -5.3×-2.6

22) -2.8×1.3

23) -8.344×5.34

24) 0.475×-9.8

25) 5.65×-3.4

26) -9.331×2.9

27) 3.7×-8.9

28) -6.9×5.5

29) -8.4×0.729

30) 2.7×-9.586

31) -0.5×3.4

32) -9.4×1.4

33) -0.4×-4.8

34) -7×-8.7

35) -1.4×3.5

36) 7.7×-2.7

37) -2.9×-8.8

38) -4.1×-3.516

39) −4.4 × −0.6

40) 5.1 × −1.98

41) −5.4 × 1.12

42) 1.574 × −2.75

43) −7 × −4.6

44) −7.3 × −9.3

45) −8.5 × 3.1

46) 1.1 × −3

47) −9.5 × −8.7

48) −0.5 × 5.2

49) 9.1 × −1

50) −1.5 × −6.6

Answers to Chapter 3 Questions: Multiplying Decimal Numbers

1) 15.51
2) −14.72
3) 0.92
4) 41.024
5) −4.44
6) −19.5
7) 19.2537
8) −65.1644
9) 1.68
10) −34.98
11) −39.22
12) 2.21
13) 30.6
14) −0.74
15) −27.39
16) −3.48
17) 79.98
18) −7.44
19) −0.771
20) 8.45
21) 13.78
22) −3.64
23) −44.55696
24) −4.655
25) −19.21
26) −27.0599
27) −32.93
28) −37.95
29) −6.1236
30) −25.8822
31) −1.7
32) −13.16
33) 1.92
34) 60.9
35) −4.9
36) −20.79
37) 25.52
38) 14.4156
39) 2.64
40) −10.098
41) −6.048
42) −4.3285
43) 32.2
44) 67.89
45) −26.35
46) −3.3
47) 82.65
48) −2.6
49) −9.1
50) 9.9

Chapter 3 Questions: Dividing Decimal Numbers

Find each quotient.

1) 1.958 ÷ 6.1

2) 4.271 ÷ 7.3

3) 7 ÷ 0.246

4) 1.6 ÷ 5.34

5) 4.4 ÷ 3.206

6) 2.7 ÷ 2.91

7) 5.5 ÷ 6.167

8) 2.7 ÷ 8

9) 7.1 ÷ 5.6

10) 3.3 ÷ 3.1

11) 7.6 ÷ 4.4

12) 3.48 ÷ 1.9

13) 0.7 ÷ 0.7

14) 4.5 ÷ 7.5

15) 5.7 ÷ 3.9

16) 1.3 ÷ 6.3

17) 1.9 ÷ 5.1

18) 6.2 ÷ 2.7

19) 3.1 ÷ 1.4

20) 6.9 ÷ 0.2

21) 7.4 ÷ 7.1

22) 3.7 ÷ 4.6

23) 7.503 ÷ 5.9

24) 0.5 ÷ 3.4

25) 4.9 ÷ 0.9

26) 1.1 ÷ 2.2

27) 6.1 ÷ 5.4

28) 1.7 ÷ 7.8

29) 2.3 ÷ 6.6

30) 6.6 ÷ 4.1

31) 7.3 ÷ 1.7

32) 3.5 ÷ 2.9

33) 7.8 ÷ 0.5

34) 4.3 ÷ 4.98

35) 2.6 ÷ 6.079

36) 5.4 ÷ 7.14

37) 1.3 ÷ 1.038

38) 0.695 ÷ 1.2

39) 2.68 ÷ 4.7

40) 6.4 ÷ 6.8

41) 2.3 ÷ 5.6

42) 3.3 ÷ 5.6

43) 7.6 ÷ 3.2

44) 3.9 ÷ 4.4

45) 0.1 ÷ 1.9

46) 0.7 ÷ 7.6

47) 5.1 ÷ 0.7

48) 1.3 ÷ 6.4

49) 6.15 ÷ 5.2

50) 1.9 ÷ 3.9

Answers to Chapter 3 Questions: Dividing Decimal Numbers

1) 0.320983606557
2) 0.585068493151
3) 28.4552845528
4) 0.299625468165
5) 1.37242669994
6) 0.927835051546
7) 0.891843684125
8) 0.3375
9) 1.26785714286
10) 1.06451612903
11) 1.72727272727
12) 1.83157894737
13) 1
14) 0.6
15) 1.46153846154
16) 0.206349206349
17) 0.372549019608
18) 2.2962962963
19) 2.21428571429
20) 34.5
21) 1.04225352113
22) 0.804347826087
23) 1.27169491525
24) 0.147058823529
25) 5.44444444444
26) 0.5
27) 1.12962962963
28) 0.217948717949
29) 0.348484848485
30) 1.60975609756
31) 4.29411764706
32) 1.20689655172
33) 15.6
34) 0.863453815261
35) 0.427701924659
36) 0.756302521008
37) 1.25240847784
38) 0.579166666667
39) 0.570212765957
40) 0.941176470588
41) 0.410714285714
42) 0.589285714286
43) 2.375
44) 0.886363636364
45) 0.0526315789474
46) 0.0921052631579
47) 7.28571428571
48) 0.203125
49) 1.18269230769
50) 0.487179487179

Chapter 4 Questions: Comparing Ratios

State if each pair of ratios forms a proportion. In other words, are the two ratios equal?

1) $\dfrac{9}{12}$ and $\dfrac{3}{4}$ 	 2) $\dfrac{12}{6}$ and $\dfrac{6}{3}$

3) $\dfrac{6}{5}$ and $\dfrac{24}{20}$ 	 4) $\dfrac{30}{25}$ and $\dfrac{6}{5}$

5) $\dfrac{8}{6}$ and $\dfrac{4}{3}$ 	 6) $\dfrac{3}{6}$ and $\dfrac{15}{30}$

7) $\dfrac{16}{24}$ and $\dfrac{4}{6}$ 	 8) $\dfrac{3}{6}$ and $\dfrac{9}{18}$

9) $\dfrac{5}{6}$ and $\dfrac{20}{24}$ 	 10) $\dfrac{5}{3}$ and $\dfrac{15}{9}$

11) $\dfrac{18}{12}$ and $\dfrac{6}{3}$ 	 12) $\dfrac{24}{6}$ and $\dfrac{6}{3}$

13) $\dfrac{10}{12}$ and $\dfrac{5}{4}$ 	 14) $\dfrac{4}{3}$ and $\dfrac{20}{9}$

15) $\dfrac{3}{4}$ and $\dfrac{9}{16}$ 	 16) $\dfrac{6}{16}$ and $\dfrac{3}{4}$

17) $\dfrac{6}{3}$ and $\dfrac{36}{21}$ 18) $\dfrac{20}{8}$ and $\dfrac{5}{4}$

19) $\dfrac{5}{4}$ and $\dfrac{35}{20}$ 20) $\dfrac{6}{5}$ and $\dfrac{36}{35}$

21) $\dfrac{6}{5}$ and $\dfrac{42}{30}$ 22) $\dfrac{3}{5}$ and $\dfrac{24}{30}$

23) $\dfrac{12}{25}$ and $\dfrac{3}{5}$ 24) $\dfrac{3}{5}$ and $\dfrac{18}{25}$

25) $\dfrac{4}{5}$ and $\dfrac{28}{25}$ 26) $\dfrac{12}{18}$ and $\dfrac{4}{6}$

27) $\dfrac{10}{6}$ and $\dfrac{5}{3}$ 28) $\dfrac{12}{15}$ and $\dfrac{4}{5}$

29) $\dfrac{3}{4}$ and $\dfrac{6}{8}$ 30) $\dfrac{3}{6}$ and $\dfrac{12}{24}$

31) $\dfrac{36}{30}$ and $\dfrac{6}{5}$ 32) $\dfrac{4}{3}$ and $\dfrac{12}{9}$

33) $\dfrac{15}{12}$ and $\dfrac{5}{4}$ 34) $\dfrac{36}{24}$ and $\dfrac{6}{4}$

35) $\dfrac{30}{24}$ and $\dfrac{5}{4}$ 36) $\dfrac{6}{4}$ and $\dfrac{12}{8}$

37) $\dfrac{6}{4}$ and $\dfrac{36}{20}$

38) $\dfrac{15}{28}$ and $\dfrac{3}{4}$

39) $\dfrac{18}{40}$ and $\dfrac{3}{5}$

40) $\dfrac{4}{5}$ and $\dfrac{28}{30}$

41) $\dfrac{4}{5}$ and $\dfrac{16}{25}$

42) $\dfrac{4}{5}$ and $\dfrac{20}{35}$

43) $\dfrac{40}{36}$ and $\dfrac{5}{6}$

44) $\dfrac{8}{15}$ and $\dfrac{4}{5}$

45) $\dfrac{12}{9}$ and $\dfrac{6}{3}$

46) $\dfrac{15}{18}$ and $\dfrac{3}{6}$

47) $\dfrac{30}{20}$ and $\dfrac{6}{5}$

48) $\dfrac{3}{6}$ and $\dfrac{15}{36}$

49) $\dfrac{3}{6}$ and $\dfrac{9}{30}$

50) $\dfrac{4}{6}$ and $\dfrac{20}{18}$

Answers to Chapter 4 Questions: Comparing Ratios

1) Yes	2) Yes	3) Yes
4) Yes	5) Yes	6) Yes
7) Yes	8) Yes	9) Yes
10) Yes	11) No	12) No
13) No	14) No	15) No
16) No	17) No	18) No
19) No	20) No	21) No
22) No	23) No	24) No
25) No	26) Yes	27) Yes
28) Yes	29) Yes	30) Yes
31) Yes	32) Yes	33) Yes
34) Yes	35) Yes	36) Yes
37) No	38) No	39) No
40) No	41) No	42) No
43) No	44) No	45) No
46) No	47) No	48) No
49) No	50) No	

Chapter 4 Questions: Solving Proportions

Find the value of the variable in each proportion. Write your answers as fractions.

1) $\dfrac{p}{9} = \dfrac{4}{11}$

2) $\dfrac{7}{12} = \dfrac{2}{n}$

3) $\dfrac{7}{8} = \dfrac{5}{x}$

4) $\dfrac{b}{7} = \dfrac{9}{4}$

5) $\dfrac{9r}{7} = \dfrac{3}{4}$

6) $\dfrac{6}{x} = \dfrac{2}{5}$

7) $\dfrac{12}{6} = \dfrac{8}{n}$

8) $\dfrac{2}{a} = \dfrac{7}{9}$

9) $\dfrac{6}{4} = \dfrac{2}{v}$

10) $\dfrac{x}{3} = \dfrac{10}{11}$

11) $\dfrac{8}{7} = \dfrac{10}{x}$

12) $\dfrac{8}{7} = \dfrac{5}{k}$

13) $\dfrac{3}{10} = \dfrac{6}{a}$

14) $\dfrac{7}{p} = \dfrac{2}{9}$

15) $\dfrac{2}{3} = \dfrac{4}{x}$

16) $\dfrac{11}{n} = \dfrac{8}{3}$

17) $\dfrac{3}{2} = \dfrac{m}{11}$

18) $\dfrac{x}{5} = \dfrac{8}{7}$

19) $\dfrac{12}{6} = \dfrac{r}{10}$

20) $\dfrac{4}{b} = \dfrac{12}{4}$

21) $\dfrac{2}{12} = \dfrac{8}{n}$

22) $\dfrac{v}{11} = \dfrac{4}{7}$

23) $\dfrac{6}{2} = \dfrac{x}{12}$

24) $\dfrac{5}{10} = \dfrac{a}{7}$

25) $\dfrac{n}{2} = \dfrac{12}{7}$

26) $\dfrac{10}{12} = \dfrac{9}{k}$

27) $\dfrac{12}{8} = \dfrac{9}{x}$

28) $\dfrac{5}{x} = \dfrac{6}{3}$

29) $\dfrac{12}{5} = \dfrac{6}{n}$

30) $\dfrac{p}{9} = \dfrac{2}{6}$

31) $\dfrac{2}{m} = \dfrac{8}{2}$

32) $\dfrac{9}{4} = \dfrac{10}{x}$

33) $\dfrac{7}{8} = \dfrac{10}{n}$

34) $\dfrac{3}{b} = \dfrac{2}{6}$

35) $\dfrac{6}{r} = \dfrac{5}{10}$

36) $\dfrac{3}{8} = \dfrac{x}{7}$

37) $\dfrac{3n}{6} = \dfrac{9}{2}$

38) $\dfrac{a}{3} = \dfrac{4}{12}$

39) $\dfrac{8}{7} = \dfrac{11}{11v}$

40) $\dfrac{5}{11} = \dfrac{3}{x}$

41) $\dfrac{7}{x} = \dfrac{12}{10}$

42) $\dfrac{k}{5} = \dfrac{4}{7}$

43) $\dfrac{6}{12} = \dfrac{11}{x}$

44) $\dfrac{7}{n} = \dfrac{11}{12}$

45) $\dfrac{8}{m} = \dfrac{11}{2}$

46) $\dfrac{3}{12} = \dfrac{x}{9}$

47) $\dfrac{9}{r} = \dfrac{6}{5}$

48) $\dfrac{8}{11} = \dfrac{n}{5}$

49) $\dfrac{b}{5} = \dfrac{11}{6}$

50) $\dfrac{6}{11} = \dfrac{v}{12}$

Answers to Chapter 4 Questions: Solving Proportions

1) $\left\{\dfrac{36}{11}\right\}$
2) $\left\{\dfrac{24}{7}\right\}$
3) $\left\{\dfrac{40}{7}\right\}$
4) $\left\{\dfrac{63}{4}\right\}$
5) $\left\{\dfrac{7}{12}\right\}$
6) $\{15\}$
7) $\{4\}$
8) $\left\{\dfrac{18}{7}\right\}$
9) $\left\{\dfrac{4}{3}\right\}$
10) $\left\{\dfrac{30}{11}\right\}$
11) $\left\{\dfrac{35}{4}\right\}$
12) $\left\{\dfrac{35}{8}\right\}$
13) $\{20\}$
14) $\left\{\dfrac{63}{2}\right\}$
15) $\{6\}$
16) $\left\{\dfrac{33}{8}\right\}$
17) $\left\{\dfrac{33}{2}\right\}$
18) $\left\{\dfrac{40}{7}\right\}$
19) $\{20\}$
20) $\left\{\dfrac{4}{3}\right\}$
21) $\{48\}$
22) $\left\{\dfrac{44}{7}\right\}$
23) $\{36\}$
24) $\left\{\dfrac{7}{2}\right\}$
25) $\left\{\dfrac{24}{7}\right\}$
26) $\left\{\dfrac{54}{5}\right\}$
27) $\{6\}$
28) $\left\{\dfrac{5}{2}\right\}$
29) $\left\{\dfrac{5}{2}\right\}$
30) $\{3\}$
31) $\left\{\dfrac{1}{2}\right\}$
32) $\left\{\dfrac{40}{9}\right\}$
33) $\left\{\dfrac{80}{7}\right\}$
34) $\{9\}$
35) $\{12\}$
36) $\left\{\dfrac{21}{8}\right\}$
37) $\{9\}$
38) $\{1\}$
39) $\left\{\dfrac{7}{8}\right\}$
40) $\left\{\dfrac{33}{5}\right\}$
41) $\left\{\dfrac{35}{6}\right\}$
42) $\left\{\dfrac{20}{7}\right\}$
43) $\{22\}$
44) $\left\{\dfrac{84}{11}\right\}$
45) $\left\{\dfrac{16}{11}\right\}$
46) $\left\{\dfrac{9}{4}\right\}$
47) $\left\{\dfrac{15}{2}\right\}$
48) $\left\{\dfrac{40}{11}\right\}$

49) $\left\{\dfrac{55}{6}\right\}$ 50) $\left\{\dfrac{72}{11}\right\}$

Chapter 4 Questions: Proportions Word Problems

Answer each question and round your answer to the nearest whole number.

1) The currency in Tonga is the Pa'anga. The exchange rate is approximately 2 Pa'anga to $1. At this rate, how many Pa'anga would you get if you exchanged $4?

2) One tub of dried cranberries costs $4. How many tubs of dried cranberries can you buy for $8?

3) One package of blueberries costs $3. How many packages can you buy for $12?

4) If you can buy one bunch of fennel for $2 then how many can you buy with $4?

5) If you can buy one jar of crushed ginger for $2 then how many can you buy with $10?

6) Pranav enlarged the size of a triangle to a height of 6 in. What is the new width if it was originally 2 in tall and 4 in wide?

7) Anjali enlarged the size of a photo to a width of 10 in. What is the new height if it was originally 1 in tall and 2 in wide?

8) Kali enlarged the size of a photo to a width of 8 in. What is the new height if it was originally 4 in wide and 1 in tall?

9) The money used in Croatia is called the Kuna. The exchange rate is $1 for every 6 Kuna. Find how many Kuna you would receive if you exchanged $3.

10) Molly took a trip to Saudi Arabia. Upon leaving she decided to convert all of her Riyals back into dollars. How many dollars did she receive if she exchanged 12 Riyals at a rate of 4 Riyals = $1?

11) Willie was planning a trip to Tajikistan. Before going, he did some research and learned that the exchange rate is $1 = 3 Somoni. How many Somoni would he get if he exchanged $2?

12) The currency in Argentina is the Peso. The exchange rate is approximately 3 Pesos for $1. At this rate, how many Pesos would you get if you exchanged $4?

13) If you can buy one bunch of seedlees red grapes for $2 then how many can you buy with $16?

14) Ryan enlarged the size of a triangle to a width of 9 in. What is the new height if it was originally 4 in tall and 3 in wide?

15) Daniel reduced the size of a triangle to a width of 2 in. What is the new height if it was originally 15 in tall and 10 in wide?

16) Jennifer bought one jar of sun-dried tomatoes for $4. How many jars can Alberto buy if he has $16?

17) Nicole reduced the size of a photo to a width of 3 in. What is the new height if it was originally 12 in wide and 8 in tall?

18) A frame is 4 in wide and 1 in tall. If it is enlarged to a height of 3 in then how wide will it be?

19) Gabriella took a trip to Oman. Upon leaving she decided to convert all of her Rials back into dollars. How many dollars did she receive if she exchanged 12 Rials at a rate of $3 to 1 Rial?

20) The currency in Western Samoa is the Tala. The exchange rate is approximately $1 to 3 Tala. At this rate, how many dollars would you get if you exchanged 12 Tala?

21) The money used in Western Samoa is called the Tala. The exchange rate is $1 to 3 Tala. Find how many Tala you would receive if you exchanged $5.

22) Shanice bought one container of dried cherries for $7. How many containers can Jacob buy if he has $14?

23) If you can buy one bunch of asparagus for $2 then how many can you buy with $8?

24) If you can buy one package of raspberries for $3 then how many can you buy with $15?

25) Abhasra bought one bunch of seedlees black grapes for $2. How many bunches of seedless black grapes can Jose buy if he has $10?

26) Kim reduced the size of a triangle to a height of 3 in. What is the new width if it was originally 12 in wide and 9 in tall?

27) A triangle is 2 in wide and 3 in tall. If it is enlarged to a width of 6 in then how tall will it be?

28) A triangle is 4 in wide and 12 in tall. If it is reduced to a width of 1 in then how tall will it be?

29) The currency in Tonga is the Pa'anga. The exchange rate is approximately 2 Pa'anga for $1. At this rate, how many dollars would you get if you exchanged 8 Pa'anga?

30) If you can buy one cantaloupe for $2 then how many can you buy with $6?

31) One bunch of seedlees green grapes costs $2. How many bunches can you buy for $14?

32) The money used in the eastern Caribbean islands is called the Eastern Caribbean Dollar. The exchange rate is $1 for every 3 Eastern Caribbean Dollars. Find how many dollars you would receive if you exchanged 6 Eastern Caribbean Dollars.

33) If you can buy one bag of radishes for $2 then how many can you buy with $12?

34) A triangle is 3 in wide and 12 in tall. If it is reduced to a height of 4 in then how wide will it be?

35) A triangle is 1 in tall and 2 in wide. If it is enlarged to a height of 4 in then how wide will it be?

36) A triangle is 8 in tall and 6 in wide. If it is reduced to a width of 3 in then how tall will it be?

37) A frame is 6 in tall and 12 in wide. If it is reduced to a height of 2 in then how wide will it be?

38) The currency in Argentina is the Peso. The exchange rate is approximately $1 for every 3 Pesos. At this rate, how many dollars would you get if you exchanged 9 Pesos?

39) The money used in South Africa is called the Rand. The exchange rate is 7 Rand to $1. Find how many Rand you would receive if you exchanged $3.

40) Rob bought one honeydew melon for $4. How many honeydew melons can Stefan buy if he has $12?

41) If you can buy one package of cherry tomatoes for $3 then how many can you buy with $9?

42) A triangle is 6 in tall and 4 in wide. If it is reduced to a height of 3 in then how wide will it be?

43) Carlos was planning a trip to South Africa. Before going, he did some research and learned that the exchange rate is $1 = 7 Rand. How many Rand would he get if he exchanged $2?

44) The currency in Tonga is the Pa'anga. The exchange rate is approximately 2 Pa'anga to $1. At this rate, how many dollars would you get if you exchanged 10 Pa'anga?

45) The money used in Tonga is called the Pa'anga. The exchange rate is $1 for every 2 Pa'anga. Find how many dollars you would receive if you exchanged 12 Pa'anga.

46) If you can buy one bunch of seedlees black grapes for $2 then how many can you buy with $12?

47) If you can buy one seedless watermelon for $2 then how many can you buy with $8?

48) Jessica enlarged the size of a triangle to a width of 12 in. What is the new height if it was originally 3 in wide and 2 in tall?

49) Joe enlarged the size of a rectangle to a height of 9 in. What is the new width if it was originally 3 in tall and 1 in wide?

50) Julio reduced the size of a rectangle to a height of 2 in. What is the new width if it was originally 8 in wide and 4 in tall?

Answers to Chapter 4 Questions: Proportions Word Problems

1) 8 Pa'anga
2) 2
3) 4
4) 2
5) 5
6) 12 in
7) 5 in
8) 2 in
9) 18 Kuna
10) $3
11) 6 Somoni
12) 12 Pesos
13) 8
14) 12 in
15) 3 in
16) 4
17) 2 in
18) 12 in
19) $36
20) $4
21) 15 Tala
22) 2
23) 4
24) 5
25) 5
26) 4 in
27) 9 in
28) 3 in
29) $4
30) 3
31) 7
32) $2
33) 6
34) 1 in
35) 8 in
36) 4 in
37) 4 in
38) $3
39) 21 Rand
40) 3
41) 3
42) 2 in
43) 14 Rand
44) $5
45) $6
46) 6
47) 4
48) 8 in
49) 3 in
50) 4 in

Chapter 5 Questions: Changing Percents to Fractions

Write each of the following percents as a fraction. Write the answer as a mixed number when possible.

1) 53%   2) 99%

3) 33%   4) 95%

5) 30%   6) 10%

7) 80%   8) 88%

9) 25%   10) 67%

11) 16%   12) 75%

13) 50%   14) 45%

15) 52%   16) 850%

17) 256%   18) 630%

19) 687%   20) 489%

21) 813%   22) 13%

23) 60%   24) 15%

25) 87%   26) 28%

27) 97%   28) 96%

29) 70%   30) 78%

31) 59%   32) 24%

33) 20%   34) 760%

35) 425%   36) 625%

37) 970% 38) 235%

39) 42% 40) 90%

41) 57% 42) 38%

43) 89% 44) 47%

45) 77% 46) 41%

47) 790% 48) 111%

49) 863% 50) 238%

Answers to Chapter 5 Questions: Changing Percents to Fractions

1) $\dfrac{53}{100}$
2) $\dfrac{99}{100}$
3) $\dfrac{33}{100}$
4) $\dfrac{19}{20}$
5) $\dfrac{3}{10}$
6) $\dfrac{1}{10}$
7) $\dfrac{4}{5}$
8) $\dfrac{22}{25}$
9) $\dfrac{1}{4}$
10) $\dfrac{67}{100}$
11) $\dfrac{4}{25}$
12) $\dfrac{3}{4}$
13) $\dfrac{1}{2}$
14) $\dfrac{9}{20}$
15) $\dfrac{13}{25}$
16) $8\dfrac{1}{2}$
17) $2\dfrac{14}{25}$
18) $6\dfrac{3}{10}$
19) $6\dfrac{87}{100}$
20) $4\dfrac{89}{100}$
21) $8\dfrac{13}{100}$
22) $\dfrac{13}{100}$
23) $\dfrac{3}{5}$
24) $\dfrac{3}{20}$
25) $\dfrac{87}{100}$
26) $\dfrac{7}{25}$
27) $\dfrac{97}{100}$
28) $\dfrac{24}{25}$
29) $\dfrac{7}{10}$
30) $\dfrac{39}{50}$
31) $\dfrac{59}{100}$
32) $\dfrac{6}{25}$
33) $\dfrac{1}{5}$
34) $7\dfrac{3}{5}$
35) $4\dfrac{1}{4}$
36) $6\dfrac{1}{4}$
37) $9\dfrac{7}{10}$
38) $2\dfrac{7}{20}$
39) $\dfrac{21}{50}$
40) $\dfrac{9}{10}$
41) $\dfrac{57}{100}$
42) $\dfrac{19}{50}$
43) $\dfrac{89}{100}$
44) $\dfrac{47}{100}$
45) $\dfrac{77}{100}$
46) $\dfrac{41}{100}$
47) $7\dfrac{9}{10}$
48) $1\dfrac{11}{100}$

49) $8\frac{63}{100}$

50) $2\frac{19}{50}$

Chapter 5 Questions: Changing Fractions to Percents

Write each fraction or mixed number as a percent. Round to the nearest percent.

1) $\dfrac{5}{9}$

2) $\dfrac{73}{100}$

3) $\dfrac{43}{100}$

4) $\dfrac{58}{65}$

5) $\dfrac{3}{8}$

6) $\dfrac{7}{100}$

7) $\dfrac{13}{75}$

8) $\dfrac{25}{74}$

9) $\dfrac{2}{5}$

10) $\dfrac{29}{50}$

11) $\dfrac{1}{5}$

12) $\dfrac{1}{4}$

13) $\dfrac{3}{10}$

14) $\dfrac{4}{5}$

15) $\dfrac{1}{2}$

16) $\dfrac{11}{15}$

17) $\dfrac{57}{100}$

18) $4\dfrac{22}{25}$

19) $\dfrac{7}{100}$

20) $8\dfrac{9}{10}$

21) $8\dfrac{29}{75}$

22) $6\dfrac{1}{8}$

23) $9\dfrac{5}{18}$

24) $6\dfrac{9}{20}$

25) $\dfrac{1}{6}$

26) $\dfrac{2}{39}$

27) $\dfrac{3}{4}$

28) $\dfrac{5}{8}$

29) $\dfrac{18}{25}$

30) $\dfrac{9}{10}$

31) $\dfrac{37}{100}$

32) $\dfrac{1}{7}$

33) $\dfrac{2}{15}$

34) $\dfrac{5}{18}$

35) $\dfrac{3}{5}$

36) $\dfrac{1}{10}$

37) $\dfrac{17}{20}$

38) $8\dfrac{1}{2}$

39) $2\dfrac{19}{50}$

40) $9\dfrac{1}{2}$

41) $5\dfrac{1}{2}$

42) $3\dfrac{1}{2}$

43) $\dfrac{9}{70}$

44) $\dfrac{32}{33}$

45) $\dfrac{27}{100}$

46) $\dfrac{1}{15}$

47) $\dfrac{1}{8}$

48) $\dfrac{23}{35}$

49) $\dfrac{59}{75}$

50) $\dfrac{19}{20}$

Answers to Chapter 5 Questions: Changing Fractions to Percents

1) 56%   2) 73%   3) 43%
4) 89%   5) 38%   6) 7%
7) 17%   8) 34%   9) 4%
10) 58%   11) 2%   12) 25%
13) 3%   14) 8%   15) 5%
16) 73%   17) 57%   18) 488%
19) 7%   20) 89%   21) 839%
22) 613%   23) 928%   24) 645%
25) 17%   26) 5%   27) 75%
28) 63%   29) 72%   30) 9%
31) 37%   32) 14%   33) 13%
34) 28%   35) 6%   36) 1%
37) 85%   38) 85%   39) 238%
40) 95%   41) 55%   42) 35%
43) 13%   44) 97%   45) 27%
46) 7%   47) 13%   48) 66%
49) 79%   50) 95%

Chapter 5 Questions: Changing Percents to Decimals

Write each percent as a decimal. Round to the nearest hundredths.

1) 97% 2) 18%

3) 40% 4) 72%

5) 5% 6) 21%

7) 3% 8) 59%

9) 13% 10) 24%

11) 43% 12) 595%

13) 859% 14) 316%

15) 223% 16) 743%

17) 107% 18) 41%

19) 60% 20) 96%

21) 71% 22) 36%

23) 82% 24) 4%

25) 47% 26) 830%

27) 77% 28) 42%

29) 53% 30) 88%

31) 1% 32) 64%

33) 29% 34) 83%

35) 2% 36) 98%

37) 70% 38) 35%

39) 809%   40) 430%
41) 299%   42) 173%
43) 436%   44) 7%
45) 87%   46) 52%
47) 17%   48) 63%
49) 28%   50) 30%

Answers to Chapter 5 Questions: Changing Percents to Decimals

1) 0.97
2) 0.18
3) 0.4
4) 0.72
5) 0.05
6) 0.21
7) 0.03
8) 0.59
9) 0.13
10) 0.24
11) 0.43
12) 5.95
13) 8.59
14) 3.16
15) 2.23
16) 7.43
17) 1.07
18) 0.41
19) 0.6
20) 0.96
21) 0.71
22) 0.36
23) 0.82
24) 0.04
25) 0.47
26) 8.3
27) 0.77
28) 0.42
29) 0.53
30) 0.88
31) 0.01
32) 0.64
33) 0.29
34) 0.83
35) 0.02
36) 0.98
37) 0.7
38) 0.35
39) 8.09
40) 4.3
41) 2.99
42) 1.73
43) 4.36
44) 0.07
45) 0.87
46) 0.52
47) 0.17
48) 0.63
49) 0.28
50) 0.3

Chapter 5 Questions: Changing Decimals to Percents

Write each decimal number as a percent. Round to the nearest tenth of a percent.

1) 0.58

2) 0.93

3) 0.813

4) 0.06

5) 0.776

6) 0.34

7) 0.9

8) 0.45

9) 0.64

10) 0.21

11) 1.189

12) 0.01

13) 0.29

14) 6.5

15) 7.25

16) 0.002

17) 0.003

18) 3.97

19) 1.87

20) 0.005

21) 0.007

22) 3.447

23) 0.564

24) 0.33

25) 0.08

26) 0.98

27) 0.19

28) 0.63

29) 0.417

30) 0.535

31) 0.85

32) 0.5

33) 0.61

34) 0.14

35) 0.05

36) 0.8

37) 0.388

38) 0.1

39) 0.001

40) 0.04

41) 4.69

42) 5.44

43) 0.004

44) 6.795

45) 0.006

46) 5.77

47) 2.49

48) 1.811

49) 0.6

50) 0.24

Answers to Chapter 5 Questions: Changing Decimals to Percents

1) 58%
2) 93%
3) 81.3%
4) 6%
5) 77.6%
6) 34%
7) 90%
8) 45%
9) 64%
10) 21%
11) 118.9%
12) 1%
13) 29%
14) 650%
15) 725%
16) 0.2%
17) 0.3%
18) 397%
19) 187%
20) 0.5%
21) 0.7%
22) 344.7%
23) 56.4%
24) 33%
25) 8%
26) 98%
27) 19%
28) 63%
29) 41.7%
30) 53.5%
31) 85%
32) 50%
33) 61%
34) 14%
35) 5%
36) 80%
37) 38.8%
38) 10%
39) 0.1%
40) 4%
41) 469%
42) 544%
43) 0.4%
44) 679.5%
45) 0.6%
46) 577%
47) 249%
48) 181.1%
49) 60%
50) 24%

Chapter 5 Questions: Calculating The Percent of Change

Find each percent change. Round to the nearest percent. State if it is an increase or decrease.

1) From 50 to 27

2) From 97 to 39

3) From 11 to 12

4) From 39 to 51.5

5) From 72.8 to 59

6) From 87 to 21

7) From 28.3 to 2.3

8) From 32 to 16

9) From 63 to 58

10) From 38 to 76

11) From 41 to 72

12) From 45 to 36

13) From 48 to 33

14) From 51.2 to 5

15) From 54 to 93

16) From 70 to 76

17) From 61 to 53

18) From 64 to 17

19) From 68 to 14

20) From 65 to 40

21) From 71 to 78

22) From 77 to 70.8

23) From 81 to 34

24) From 84 to 30

25) From 87 to 95

26) From 70 to 34

27) From 94 to 55

28) From 97 to 51

29) From 100 to 15

30) From 66 to 13

31) From 100 to 57

32) From 22 to 9

33) From 17 to 32

34) From 36 to 21

35) From 20 to 28

36) From 22 to 18

37) From 30 to 53

38) From 53.5 to 65

39) From 33 to 49

40) From 36 to 13

41) From 43 to 73

42) From 39 to 9

43) From 46 to 70

44) From 49 to 66

45) From 52 to 30.1

46) From 56.2 to 99

47) From 59 to 90

48) From 62.2 to 58

49) From 66 to 51

50) From 69 to 47

Answers to Chapter 5 Questions: Calculating The Percent of Change

1) 46% decrease
2) 60% decrease
3) 9% increase
4) 32% increase
5) 19% decrease
6) 76% decrease
7) 92% decrease
8) 50% decrease
9) 8% decrease
10) 100% increase
11) 76% increase
12) 20% decrease
13) 31% decrease
14) 90% decrease
15) 72% increase
16) 9% increase
17) 13% decrease
18) 73% decrease
19) 79% decrease
20) 38% decrease
21) 10% increase
22) 8% decrease
23) 58% decrease
24) 64% decrease
25) 9% increase
26) 51% decrease
27) 41% decrease
28) 47% decrease
29) 85% decrease
30) 80% decrease
31) 43% decrease
32) 59% decrease
33) 88% increase
34) 42% decrease
35) 40% increase
36) 18% decrease
37) 77% increase
38) 21% increase
39) 48% increase
40) 64% decrease
41) 70% increase
42) 77% decrease
43) 52% increase
44) 35% increase
45) 42% decrease
46) 76% increase
47) 53% increase
48) 7% decrease
49) 23% decrease
50) 32% decrease

Chapter 5 Questions: Value After Markup OR Discount

Find the selling price of each item after a markup or discount (as indicated in each question).

1) Cost of concert tickets: $200.00
   Markup: 25%

2) Cost of socks: $4.99
   Markup: 94%

3) Cost of a bicycle: $1,600.00
   Markup: 19%

4) Cost of a radio: $36.95
   Markup: 90%

5) Cost of a comb: $3.40
   Markup: 30%

6) Cost of a telescope: $619.50
   Markup: 80%

7) Cost of a kitten: $49.95
   Markup: 30%

8) Cost of a lizard: $14.99
   Markup: 10%

9) Cost of a sled: $50.00
   Markup: 45%

10) Cost of a purse: $144.50
    Markup: 40%

11) Cost of a shirt: $62.00
    Markup: 20%

12) Cost of a cell phone: $249.95
    Markup: 30%

13) Cost of concert tickets: $199.50
    Markup: 60%

14) Cost of socks: $26.50
    Markup: 15%

15) Cost of a bicycle: $1,000.00
    Markup: 25%

16) Cost of a radio: $20.50
    Markup: 85%

17) Cost of a comb: $3.85
    Markup: 90%

18) Cost of a telescope: $209.95
    Markup: 5%

19) Cost of a kitten: $60.00
    Markup: 30%

20) Cost of a sled: $90.00
    Markup: 38%

21) Cost of a lizard: $34.99
    Markup: 79%

22) Cost of shoes: $119.95
    Markup: 91%

23) Cost of a cell phone: $199.99
    Markup: 85%

24) Cost of a shirt: $57.00
    Markup: 5%

25) Cost of concert tickets: $99.50
    Markup: 84%

26) Original price of concert tickets: $89.50
    Discount: 30%

27) Original price of a computer: $3,800.00
    Discount: 38%

28) Original price of socks: $14.95
    Discount: 37%

29) Original price of an SUV: $19,000.00
    Discount: 30%

30) Original price of a comb: $3.50
    Discount: 5%

31) Original price of a CD: $11.95
    Discount: 20%

32) Original price of a telescope: $700.00
    Discount: 53%

33) Original price of a puppy: $389.95
    Discount: 30%

34) Original price of a sled: $169.95
    Discount: 10%

35) Original price of a goldfish: $1.75
    Discount: 50%

36) Original price of a purse: $99.50
    Discount: 20%

37) Original price of pants: $50.00
    Discount: 10%

38) Original price of a cell phone: $205.00
    Discount: 25%

39) Original price of concert tickets: $49.50
    Discount: 10%

40) Original price of socks: $25.50
    Discount: 30%

41) Original price of an SUV: $13,700.00
    Discount: 48%

42) Original price of a radio: $10.99
    Discount: 40%

43) Original price of a comb: $2.95
    Discount: 20%

44) Original price of a telescope: $269.99
    Discount: 50%

45) Original price of a puppy: $114.50
    Discount: 5%

46) Original price of a lizard: $4.99
    Discount: 50%

47) Original price of a sled: $149.50
    Discount: 20%

48) Original price of a purse: $184.95
    Discount: 30%

49) Original price of pants: $69.50
    Discount: 10%

50) Original price of a cell phone: $219.50
    Discount: 20%

Answers to Chapter 5 Questions: Value After Markup OR Discount

1) $250.00
2) $9.68
3) $1,904.00
4) $70.20
5) $4.42
6) $1,115.10
7) $64.94
8) $16.49
9) $72.50
10) $202.30
11) $74.40
12) $324.94
13) $319.20
14) $30.47
15) $1,250.00
16) $37.93
17) $7.31
18) $220.45
19) $78.00
20) $124.20
21) $62.63
22) $229.10
23) $369.98
24) $59.85
25) $183.08
26) $62.65
27) $2,356.00
28) $9.42
29) $13,300.00
30) $3.32
31) $9.56
32) $329.00
33) $272.96
34) $152.95
35) $0.88
36) $79.60
37) $45.00
38) $153.75
39) $44.55
40) $17.85
41) $7,124.00
42) $6.59
43) $2.36
44) $135.00
45) $108.77
46) $2.50
47) $119.60
48) $129.46
49) $62.55
50) $175.60

Math Practice by Kareem Gouda   www.SKOOLOO.com

Chapter 5 Questions: Value After Two Successive Changes

Find the selling price of each item after two successive changes (Markup & Discount) in the order given in the questions.

1) Cost of a tie: $20.50
   Markup: 80%
   Discount: 55%

2) Cost of a bicycle: $1,900.00
   Markup: 60%
   Discount: 40%

3) Cost of a radio: $74.99
   Markup: 80%
   Discount: 10%

4) Cost of a comb: $1.50
   Markup: 70%
   Discount: 40%

5) Cost of a microscope: $234.95
   Markup: 30%
   Discount: 25%

6) Cost of a lizard: $44.95
   Markup: 8%
   Discount: 29%

7) Cost of a kitten: $110.00
   Markup: 40%
   Discount: 31%

8) Cost of a sled: $119.99
   Markup: 90%
   Discount: 20%

9) Cost of shoes: $54.99
   Markup: 19%
   Discount: 10%

10) Cost of a shirt: $44.95
    Markup: 23%
    Discount: 50%

11) Cost of a cell phone: $99.50
    Markup: 16%
    Discount: 18%

12) Cost of an MP3 player: $249.99
    Markup: 70%
    Discount: 21%

13) Cost of a tie: $28.99
    Markup: 5%
    Discount: 5%

14) Cost of a bicycle: $1,700.00
    Markup: 40%
    Discount: 42%

15) Cost of a radio: $9.99
    Markup: 54%
    Discount: 30%

16) Cost of an oil change: $24.99
    Markup: 85%
    Discount: 30%

17) Cost of a microscope: $299.50
    Markup: 10%
    Discount: 45%

18) Cost of a kitten: $89.50
    Markup: 5%
    Discount: 40%

19) Cost of a lizard: $41.50
    Markup: 90%
    Discount: 20%

20) Cost of a sweater: $13.99
    Markup: 60%
    Discount: 30%

21) Cost of shoes: $109.95
    Markup: 60%
    Discount: 15%

22) Cost of a shirt: $29.95
    Markup: 15%
    Discount: 18%

23) Cost of a cell phone: $220.00
    Markup: 20%
    Discount: 10%

24) Cost of an MP3 player: $199.50
    Markup: 43%
    Discount: 44%

25) Cost of a tie: $5.95
    Markup: 10%
    Discount: 20%

26) Cost of a jacket: $49.95
    Markup: 5%
    Discount: 20%

27) Cost of a bicycle: $499.50
    Markup: 95%
    Discount: 10%

28) Cost of a microscope: $150.00
    Markup: 45%
    Discount: 50%

29) Cost of an oil change: $33.50
    Markup: 78%
    Discount: 11%

30) Cost of a kitten: $49.99
    Markup: 40%
    Discount: 55%

31) Cost of a pen: $2.50
    Markup: 30%
    Discount: 40%

32) Cost of a sweater: $41.99
    Markup: 30%
    Discount: 20%

33) Cost of shoes: $140.00
    Markup: 26%
    Discount: 10%

34) Cost of a shirt: $49.50
    Markup: 82%
    Discount: 10%

35) Cost of a camera: $239.50
    Markup: 47%
    Discount: 25%

36) Cost of an MP3 player: $149.99
    Markup: 50%
    Discount: 50%

37) Cost of a tie: $24.95
    Markup: 20%
    Discount: 10%

38) Cost of a bicycle: $1,200.00
    Markup: 30%
    Discount: 15%

39) Cost of an oil change: $31.50
    Markup: 20%
    Discount: 15%

40) Cost of a jacket: $399.95
    Markup: 80%
    Discount: 20%

41) Cost of a microscope: $259.95
    Markup: 45%
    Discount: 50%

42) Cost of a parrot: $529.50
    Markup: 40%
    Discount: 15%

43) Cost of a pen: $1.50
    Markup: 95%
    Discount: 15%

44) Cost of a sweater: $19.99
    Markup: 45%
    Discount: 10%

45) Cost of shoes: $149.99
    Markup: 20%
    Discount: 60%

46) Cost of a car: $7,500.00
    Markup: 45%
    Discount: 40%

47) Cost of a camera: $269.95
    Markup: 30%
    Discount: 10%

48) Cost of an MP3 player: $60.00
    Markup: 70%
    Discount: 20%

49) Cost of a tie: $9.95
    Markup: 75%
    Discount: 31%

50) Cost of a motorcycle: $2,000.00
    Markup: 30%
    Discount: 43%

Answers to Chapter 5 Questions: Value After Two Successive Changes

1) $16.60	2) $1,824.00	3) $121.48
4) $1.53	5) $229.08	6) $34.47
7) $106.26	8) $182.38	9) $58.89
10) $27.64	11) $94.64	12) $335.74
13) $28.92	14) $1,380.40	15) $10.77
16) $32.36	17) $181.20	18) $56.39
19) $63.08	20) $15.67	21) $149.53
22) $28.24	23) $237.60	24) $159.76
25) $5.24	26) $41.96	27) $876.62
28) $108.75	29) $53.07	30) $31.49
31) $1.95	32) $43.67	33) $158.76
34) $81.08	35) $264.05	36) $112.49
37) $26.95	38) $1,326.00	39) $32.13
40) $575.93	41) $188.46	42) $630.10
43) $2.49	44) $26.09	45) $72.00
46) $6,525.00	47) $315.84	48) $81.60
49) $12.01	50) $1,482.00	

Chapter 5 Questions: Common Percent Problems

Solve each problem.

1) 23% of 65 is what?

2) What is 12% of 7.8?

3) 2% of 77 is what?

4) 56% of 2 is what?

5) What is 19% of 59.1?

6) What is 46% of 71.5?

7) What is 82% of 7?

8) What is 37% of 12?

9) 27% of 33 is what?

10) 18% of 23 is what?

11) 72% of 28 is what?

12) What is 63% of 49.3?

13) What is 155% of 76?

14) 390% of 12 is what?

15) What is 150% of 27?

16) What is 290% of 10?

17) 350% of 26 is what?

18) 140% of 41 is what?

19) What is 79% of 75?

20) What is 24% of 70?

21) What percent of 76 is 7?

22) 10 is what percent of 52?

23) 14 is what percent of 77?

24) 17 is what percent of 53?

25) What percent of 77 is 20?

26) What percent of 24.5 is 19.6?

27) What percent of 77.1 is 27?

28) What percent of 18 is 30.4?

29) What percent of 78 is 33?

30) What percent of 54 is 37?

31) 40 is what percent of 78?

32) What percent of 54 is 43?

33) What percent of 63 is 46.3?

34) What percent of 54.8 is 50?

35) 31 is what percent of 53?

36) 63 is 47% of what?

37) 92% of what is 10?

38) 29% of what is 154?

39) 82% of what is 159?

40) 139 is 67% of what?

41) 73% of what is 20.6?

42) 94 is 18% of what?

43) 9 is 63% of what?

44) 55 is 280% of what?

45) 152% of what is 150?

46) 180% of what is 54?

47) 149 is 113% of what?

48) 390% of what is 84?

49) 20 is 230% of what?

50) 147 is 79% of what?

Answers to Chapter 5 Questions: Common Percent Problems

1) 15
2) 0.94
3) 1.54
4) 1.12
5) 11.2
6) 32.9
7) 5.7
8) 4.4
9) 8.9
10) 4.1
11) 20.2
12) 31.1
13) 117.8
14) 46.8
15) 40.5
16) 29
17) 91
18) 57.4
19) 59.3
20) 16.8
21) 9.2%
22) 19.2%
23) 18.2%
24) 32.1%
25) 26%
26) 80%
27) 35%
28) 168.9%
29) 42.3%
30) 68.5%
31) 51.3%
32) 79.6%
33) 73.5%
34) 91.2%
35) 58.5%
36) 134
37) 10.9
38) 531
39) 193.9
40) 207.5
41) 28.2
42) 522.2
43) 14.3
44) 19.6
45) 98.7
46) 30
47) 131.9
48) 21.5
49) 8.7
50) 186.1

Chapter 9 Questions: Combining Like Terms

Combine the like terms. That means add or subtract the variables together and the numbers together. Example: The answer to number 1 would be 6m + 1 because 4m + 2m is 6m and 3-2 is 1.

1) $4m + 2m + 3 - 2$

2) $1 - 7n + 1 + 8n$

3) $-b + 10b$

4) $-8v - 2v$

5) $4x + 7 + 6$

6) $-9n - n$

7) $-6a - 9 - 10a + 8$

8) $4k + 7k$

9) $3p - 5 - 9$

10) $1 + 7x + 8x$

11) $m - 9 - 8$

12) $-4n + 4n$

13) $-5r + 4r$

14) $x - 4 - 3x - 7$

15) $-5n - 10n$

16) $5b + 8 - 2$

17) $-5x - 7x$

18) $10 + 4v + v + 4$

19) $n - 2 + 4n + 3$

20) $2a - 4 + 5a$

21) $7v + 9 + 10$

22) $-x - 6x$

23) $7n + 5 - 7n - 2$

24) $5x + 5x$

25) $4k + 4k$

26) $-2p + 2p$

27) $5x + 9 - 1$

28) $-3n + n$

29) $9r + 9r$

30) $-8m - 7 + 7m - 2$

31) $x + 1 - 3x$

32) $2n + 10 + 3$

33) $2b - 2b$

34) $v + 6 + v - 8$

35) $x + 6x$

36) $a - 8a$

37) $-6x - 2 - 4 - 7x$

38) $7k + 2k$

39) $6x + 2x$

40) $8p + 2 + 1 + 2p$

41) $9 + 6n + 6n - 7$

42) $5m + 10m$

43) $r + 4 - 10$

44) $9x + 3 + 1$

45) $-10n + 7n$

46) $b + 10 + 10b - 4$

47) $10v + 6v$

48) $1 - 2x - 10$

49) $10n - 7n$

50) $3a + 3a$

Answers to Chapter 9 Questions: Combining Like Terms

1) $6m + 1$
2) $2 + n$
3) $9b$
4) $-10v$
5) $4x + 13$
6) $-10n$
7) $-16a - 1$
8) $11k$
9) $3p - 14$
10) $1 + 15x$
11) $m - 17$
12) 0
13) $-r$
14) $-2x - 11$
15) $-15n$
16) $5b + 6$
17) $-12x$
18) $14 + 5v$
19) $5n + 1$
20) $7a - 4$
21) $7v + 19$
22) $-7x$
23) 3
24) $10x$
25) $8k$
26) 0
27) $5x + 8$
28) $-2n$
29) $18r$
30) $-m - 9$
31) $-2x + 1$
32) $2n + 13$
33) 0
34) $2v - 2$
35) $7x$
36) $-7a$
37) $-13x - 6$
38) $9k$
39) $8x$
40) $10p + 3$
41) $2 + 12n$
42) $15m$
43) $r - 6$
44) $9x + 4$
45) $-3n$
46) $11b + 6$
47) $16v$
48) $-9 - 2x$
49) $3n$
50) $6a$

Chapter 9 Questions: Evaluating Expressions

Evaluate each using the values given by substituting each variable with the numbers given.

1) $b^3 - a$; use $a = 4$, and $b = 3$

2) $(x - y)^2$; use $x = 3$, and $y = 1$

3) $j - h \div 6$; use $h = 6$, and $j = 3$

4) $2n + m$; use $m = 3$, and $n = 6$

5) $3x - y$; use $x = 3$, and $y = 6$

6) $x^2 y$; use $x = 2$, and $y = 2$

7) $m - (q - q)$; use $m = 5$, and $q = 5$

8) $pq - q$; use $p = 2$, and $q = 4$

9) $x(x + y)$; use $x = 5$, and $y = 4$

10) $h + j + h$; use $h = 2$, and $j = 1$

11) $y - (4 - x)$; use $x = 4$, and $y = 1$

12) $a(b + a)$; use $a = 6$, and $b = 3$

13) $j + 3 + h$; use $h = 1$, and $j = 3$

14) $n - (n - m)$; use $m = 6$, and $n = 6$

15) $1 + m + p$; use $m = 6$, and $p = 2$

16) $(x + z)^2$; use $x = 2$, and $z = 3$

17) $y - (y - x)$; use $x = 3$, and $y = 5$

18) $p + q^2$; use $p = 5$, and $q = 4$

19) $x - y \div 4$; use $x = 5$, and $y = 4$

20) $y - (y - x)$; use $x = 2$, and $y = 6$

21) $h - (h - k)$; use $h = 4$, and $k = 4$

22) $b - (a - a)$; use $a = 1$, and $b = 3$

23) $2x - z$; use $x = 4$, and $z = 1$

24) $j - (4 - h)$; use $h = 3$, and $j = 3$

25) $y \div 5 + x$; use $x = 4$, and $y = 5$

26) pm^3; use $m = 2$, and $p = 2$

27) $n + m - m$; use $m = 6$, and $n = 5$

28) $x + yx$; use $x = 3$, and $y = 2$

29) $4 + y + x$; use $x = 2$, and $y = 4$

30) $4xy$; use $x = 2$, and $y = 6$

31) $4 + p - q$; use $p = 5$, and $q = 4$

32) $q(q - p)$; use $p = 4$, and $q = 6$

33) $3bc$; use $b = 3$, and $c = 5$

34) $h + j + 1$; use $h = 4$, and $j = 3$

35) $(x - y)^3$; use $x = 6$, and $y = 5$

36) $x + z - z$; use $x = 1$, and $z = 4$

37) $q - p^2$; use $p = 2$, and $q = 6$

38) $m + n - n$; use $m = 6$, and $n = 5$

39) $x - y + x$; use $x = 5$, and $y = 2$

40) $q + q + p$; use $p = 2$, and $q = 4$

41) $x + y^2$; use $x = 2$, and $y = 4$

42) $yx \div 6$; use $x = 5$, and $y = 6$

43) $5(q - p)$; use $p = 1$, and $q = 6$

44) $b + a - b$; use $a = 4$, and $b = 3$

45) $(h - k)^2$; use $h = 6$, and $k = 3$

46) $m(n + n)$; use $m = 3$, and $n = 5$

47) $(m - p) \div 4$; use $m = 5$, and $p = 1$

48) $y(y + x)$; use $x = 1$, and $y = 5$

49) $q + p + p$; use $p = 2$, and $q = 4$

50) $x - y \div 2$; use $x = 6$, and $y = 2$

Answers to Chapter 9 Questions: Evaluating Expressions

1) 23	2) 4	3) 2
4) 15	5) 3	6) 8
7) 5	8) 4	9) 45
10) 5	11) 1	12) 54
13) 7	14) 6	15) 9
16) 25	17) 3	18) 21
19) 4	20) 2	21) 4
22) 3	23) 7	24) 2
25) 5	26) 16	27) 5
28) 9	29) 10	30) 48
31) 5	32) 12	33) 45
34) 8	35) 1	36) 1
37) 2	38) 6	39) 8
40) 10	41) 18	42) 5
43) 25	44) 4	45) 9
46) 30	47) 1	48) 30
49) 8	50) 5	

Math Practice by KareemGouda www.SKOOLOO.com

Chapter 9 Questions: One Step Equations

Solve each equation. Use the rules of simplifying using addition, subtraction, multiplication, and division.

1) $n + 2 = 9$

2) $b + 4 = 0$

3) $r + 2 = 8$

4) $\dfrac{x}{5} = 5$

5) $n - 3 = -10$

6) $x - 4 = 0$

7) $3a = 9$

8) $9v = 9$

9) $2x = -20$

10) $\dfrac{x}{9} = -4$

11) $8 + k = 16$

12) $\dfrac{a}{2} = 6$

13) $1 + p = -2$

14) $x + 7 = 14$

15) $n - 3 = -5$

16) $m - 7 = -13$

17) $4r = 24$

18) $6x = -36$

19) $-9n = -36$

20) $\dfrac{v}{10} = 8$

21) $x + 5 = 6$

22) $4 + a = 13$

23) $n + 10 = 0$

24) $p - 3 = 5$

25) $k - 10 = -12$

26) $9x = 45$

27) $3n = -15$

28) $\dfrac{p}{6} = 6$

29) $\dfrac{x}{8} = -1$

30) $n + 7 = 9$

31) $7 + b = -2$

32) $r - 7 = -5$

33) $x - 7 = -8$

34) $n - 8 = 1$

35) $-9v = -81$

36) $6a = -6$

37) $\dfrac{x}{6} = -5$

38) $\dfrac{x}{9} = -8$

39) $k + 10 = 13$

40) $\dfrac{n}{3} = -10$

41) $x - 10 = -7$

42) $p + 4 = -3$

43) $n - 4 = -12$

44) $m - 10 = 0$

45) $-5r = 0$

46) $9x = 90$

47) $\dfrac{n}{6} = -6$

48) $\dfrac{b}{8} = -9$

49) $\dfrac{v}{6} = -4$

50) $x + 4 = 5$

Answers to Chapter 9 Questions: One Step Equations

1) {7}
2) {−4}
3) {6}
4) {25}
5) {−7}
6) {4}
7) {3}
8) {1}
9) {−10}
10) {−36}
11) {8}
12) {12}
13) {−3}
14) {7}
15) {−2}
16) {−6}
17) {6}
18) {−6}
19) {4}
20) {80}
21) {1}
22) {9}
23) {−10}
24) {8}
25) {−2}
26) {5}
27) {−5}
28) {36}
29) {−8}
30) {2}
31) {−9}
32) {2}
33) {−1}
34) {9}
35) {9}
36) {−1}
37) {−30}
38) {−72}
39) {3}
40) {−30}
41) {3}
42) {−7}
43) {−8}
44) {10}
45) {0}
46) {10}
47) {−36}
48) {−72}
49) {−24}
50) {1}

Chapter 9 Questions: Easy Word Problems

1) Jessica spent $80 on ten toy cars. How much did each toy car cost?

2) If the weight of a package is multiplied by $\frac{7}{9}$ the result is 50.4 pounds. Find the weight of the package.

3) At a restaurant, Stefan and his three friends decided to divide the bill evenly. If each person paid $17.67 then what was the total bill?

4) Six workers are hired to harvest strawberries from a field. Each is given a plot which is 8×6 feet in size. What is the total area of the field?

5) Jill ran 18 miles less than Lea last week. Jill ran 18 miles. How many miles did Lea run?

6) Last week Totsakan ran 16 miles less than Julio. Totsakan ran 10 miles. How many miles did Julio run?

7) Elisa paid $9 for a salad. She now has $18. How much money did she have before buying the salad?

8) In six years Joe will be 43 years old. How old is he now?

9) Rob wants to buy an MP3 player for $131.73. He gives the cashier $200. How much change does he receive?

10) For babysitting Ashley was given $18.66. Now she has $27.87. How much money did she have before?

11) Last week Molly ran 34.1 miles more than Bill. Molly ran 45.4 miles. How many miles did Bill run?

12) Sumalee is cooking muffins. The recipe calls for 3 cups of sugar. She accidentally put in 8 cups. How many extra cups did she put in?

13) Shawna is cooking a casserole. The recipe calls for $4\frac{3}{5}$ cups of rice. She accidentally put in $5\frac{5}{8}$ cups. How many extra cups did she put in?

14) Eduardo won 60 super bouncy balls playing horseshoes at the county fair. At school he gave one to every student in his math class. He only has 35 remaining. How many did he give away?

15) Last week Jenny ran 15 miles less than DeShawn. Jenny ran 9 miles. How many miles did DeShawn run?

16) John ran 28 miles less than Alberto last week. John ran 17 miles. How many miles did Alberto run?

17) Shanice paid $6.07 for a salad. She now has $37.26. How much money did she have before buying the salad?

18) Gabriella will be 41 years old in twenty years. How old is she now?

19) A recipe for muffins calls for $4\frac{1}{3}$ cups of sugar. Mofor has already put in $2\frac{1}{6}$ cups. How many more cups does he need to put in?

20) Jaidee and her best friend found some money buried in a field. They split the money evenly, each getting $29. How much money did they find?

21) Find the price of one pen if nine pens cost $36.

22) A stray dog ate 27 of your muffins. That was $\frac{3}{4}$ of all of them! With how many did you start?

23) Mary and seven of her friends went out to eat. They decided to split the bill evenly. Each person paid $15. What was the total bill?

24) Willie spent $33.30 on five colored markers. How much did each marker cost?

25) If the weight of a package is multiplied by $\frac{3}{4}$ the result is 19.2 pounds. Find the weight of the package.

26) The wind blew away 15 of your muffins. That was $\frac{3}{7}$ of all of them! How many are left?

27) Four workers are hired to harvest strawberries from a field. Each is given a plot which is 11×9 feet in size. What is the total area of the field?

28) Your uncle gave you $1.08 with which to buy a present. This covered $\frac{3}{8}$ of the cost. How much did the present cost?

29) A mean ogre stole 15 of your muffins. That was $\frac{5}{6}$ of all of them! How many are left?

30) Matt and his best friend found some money in an envelope. They split the money evenly, each getting $21. How much money did they find?

31) Trevon spent $32 on cereal. If they cost $8 / box, how many boxes did he buy?

32) A hungry elf ate 40 of your muffins. That was $\frac{5}{6}$ of all of them! With how many did you start?

33) Krystal and nine of her friends went out to eat. They decided to split the bill evenly. Each person paid $11.06. What was the total bill?

34) Diapers cost $7 / package. How many packages did Kali buy if she spent $56?

35) Nicole won 65 super bouncy balls playing the bean bag toss. After giving some away she only has 42 remaining. How many did she give away?

36) Jack ran 9 miles less than Shawna last week. Jack ran 15 miles. How many miles did Shawna run?

37) Eighteen years ago, Huong was 13 years old. How old is she now?

38) Micaela paid $2 for a pizza. She now has $30. With how much money did she start?

39) Maria is cooking a casserole. The recipe calls for $3\frac{3}{4}$ cups of rice. She has already put in $3\frac{2}{5}$ cups. How many more cups does she need to put in?

40) Ming ran 25.7 miles more than Pranav last week. Ming ran 44.1 miles. How many miles did Pranav run?

41) Chelsea wants to buy a puppy for $116.83. She gives the cashier $120. What is her change?

42) Perry wants to buy an MP3 player that costs $87. How much change does he receive if he gives the cashier $100?

43) For washing the car Norachai was given $11. Now he has $27. How much money did he have before?

44) A recipe for cookies calls for $5\frac{1}{5}$ cups of sugar. Krystal has already put in $4\frac{3}{4}$ cups. How many more cups does she need to put in?

45) Carlos won 50 lollipops playing hoops. After giving some away he only has 33 remaining. How many did he give away?

46) Jennifer was 14 years old fifteen years ago. How old is she now?

47) Jose is cooking muffins. The recipe calls for 7 cups of sugar. He accidentally put in 9 cups. How many extra cups did he put in?

48) After paying $8.98 for a pizza, Aliyah has $30. With how much money did she start?

49) Ashley ran 22.1 miles less than Kim last week. Ashley ran 7 miles. How many miles did Kim run?

50) Nine workers are hired to harvest strawberries from a field. Each is given a plot which is 6×11 feet in size. What is the total area of the field?

Answers to Chapter 9 Questions: Easy Word Problems

1) $8
2) 64.8
3) $70.68
4) 288
5) 36
6) 26
7) $27
8) 37
9) $68.27
10) $9.21
11) 11.3
12) 5
13) $1\frac{1}{40}$
14) 25
15) 24
16) 45
17) $43.33
18) 21
19) $2\frac{1}{6}$
20) $58
21) $4
22) 36
23) $120
24) $6.66
25) 25.6
26) 20
27) 396
28) $2.88
29) 3
30) $42
31) 4
32) 48
33) $110.60
34) 8
35) 23
36) 24
37) 31
38) $32
39) $\frac{7}{20}$
40) 18.4
41) $3.17
42) $13
43) $16
44) $\frac{9}{20}$
45) 17
46) 29
47) 2
48) $38.98
49) 29.1
50) 594

Chapter 9 Questions: Harder Word Problems

1) The Cooking Club made some pies to sell during lunch to raise money for a field trip. The cafeteria helped by donating two pies to the club. Each pie was then cut into seven pieces and sold. There were a total of 49 pieces to sell. How many pies did the club make?

2) Aliyah wanted to make note cards by cutting pieces of paper in half. Before starting she got four more pieces to use. When she was done she had 28 half-pieces of paper. With how many pieces did she start?

3) Asanji's Bikes rents bikes for $13 plus $5 per hour. Mary paid $28 to rent a bike. For how many hours did she rent the bike?

4) Beth rented a bike from Pranav's Bikes. It cost $11 plus $4 per hour. If Beth paid $19 then she rented the bike for how many hours?

5) Jose had $22 to spend on three pencils. After buying them he had $10. How much did each pencil cost?

6) Norachai won 43 lollipops playing basketball at the county fair. At school he gave three to every student in his math class. He only has 4 remaining. How many students are in his class?

7) DeShawn had some candy to give to his four children. He first took six pieces for himself and then evenly divided the rest among his children. Each child received two pieces. With how many pieces did he start?

8) Kayla had some candy to give to her three children. She first took nine pieces for herself and then evenly divided the rest among her children. Each child received five pieces. With how many pieces did she start?

9) Ryan wanted to make note cards by cutting pieces of paper in half. Before starting he got two more pieces to use. When he was done he had 20 half-pieces of paper. With how many pieces did he start?

10) A wise man once said, "400 reduced by 3 times my age is 193." What is his age?

11) For a field trip 28 students rode in cars and the rest filled nine buses. How many students were in each bus if 226 students were on the trip?

12) The Cooking Club made some pies to sell during lunch to raise money for an end-of-year banquet. The cafeteria contributed three pies to the club. Each pie was then cut into six pieces and sold. There were a total of 48 pieces to sell. How many pies did the club make?

13) A wise man once said, "400 reduced by 3 times my age is 232." What is his age?

14) On Tuesday Perry bought ten posters. On Wednesday half of all the posters that he had were destroyed. On Thursday there were only 25 left. How many did he have on Monday?

15) The sum of three consecutive numbers is 30. What are the smallest of these numbers?

16) Stefan won 40 pieces of gum playing basketball at his school's game night. Later, he gave two to each of his friends. He only has 10 remaining. How many friends does he have?

17) Dan won 45 pieces of gum playing hoops at his school's game night. Later, he gave two to each of his friends. He only has 3 remaining. How many friends does he have?

18) Julia bought seven boxes. A week later half of all her boxes were destroyed in a fire. There are now only 19 boxes left. With how many did she start?

19) Jaidee rented a bike from Micaela's Bikes. It cost $16 plus $7 per hour. If Jaidee paid $65 then she rented the bike for how many hours?

20) Jenny had some candy to give to her five children. She first took eight pieces for herself and then evenly divided the rest among her children. Each child received five pieces. With how many pieces did she start?

21) Shanice spent $29 on a magazine and some notepads. If the magazine cost $4 and each notepad cost $5 then how many notepads did she buy?

22) Julio had some candy to give to his four children. He first took nine pieces for himself and then evenly divided the rest among his children. Each child received two pieces. With how many pieces did he start?

23) The Cooking Club made some pies to sell during lunch to raise money for an end-of-year banquet. The cafeteria contributed four pies to the club. Each pie was then cut into eight pieces and sold. There were a total of 72 pieces to sell. How many pies did the club make?

24) Amy had some candy to give to her five children. She first took two pieces for herself and then evenly divided the rest among her children. Each child received four pieces. With how many pieces did she start?

25) You had $25 to spend on four pencils. After buying them you had $9. How much did each pencil cost?

26) Cody won 71 pieces of gum playing hoops at his school's game night. Later, he gave four to each of his friends. He only has 7 remaining. How many friends does he have?

27) Ashley won 101 super bouncy balls playing hoops at her school's game night. Later, she gave four to each of her friends. She only has 9 remaining. How many friends does she have?

28) Mark wanted to make note cards by cutting pieces of paper in half. Before starting he got three more pieces to use. When he was done he had 14 half-pieces of paper. With how many pieces did he start?

29) Brenda wanted to make note cards by cutting pieces of paper in half. Before starting she got three more pieces to use. When she was done she had 20 half-pieces of paper. With how many pieces did she start?

30) Shayna had some candy to give to her four children. She first took one pieces for herself and then evenly divided the rest among her children. Each child received five pieces. With how many pieces did she start?

31) The sum of three consecutive odd numbers is 81. What are the smallest of these numbers?

32) The Cooking Club made some pies to sell at a basketball game to raise money for the new math books. The cafeteria contributed three pies to the sale. Each pie was then cut into four pieces and sold. There were a total of 32 pieces to sell. How many pies did the club make?

33) A wise man once said, "300 reduced by 3 times my age is 3." What is his age?

34) Mary had some candy to give to her five children. She first took eight pieces for herself and then evenly divided the rest among her children. Each child received four pieces. With how many pieces did she start?

35) The Cooking Club made some pies to sell at a basketball game to raise money for the new math books. The cafeteria contributed two pies to the sale. Each pie was then cut into six pieces and sold. There were a total of 60 pieces to sell. How many pies did the club make?

36) Maria won 56 super bouncy balls playing hoops at the county fair. At school she gave two to every student in her math class. She only has 6 remaining. How many students are in her class?

37) Mofor wanted to make note cards by cutting pieces of paper in half. Before starting he got five more pieces to use. When he was done he had 22 half-pieces of paper. With how many pieces did he start?

38) Huong had some paper with which to make note cards. On her way to her room she found seven more pieces to use. In her room she cut each piece of paper in half. When she was done she had 32 half-pieces of paper. With how many sheets of paper did she start?

39) Jasmine won 58 super bouncy balls playing hoops at her school's game night. Later, she gave two to each of her friends. She only has 10 remaining. How many friends does she have?

40) You bought a magazine for $5 and two notepads. You spent a total of $9. How much did each notepad cost?

41) A wise man once said, "400 reduced by 4 times my age is 16." What is his age?

42) Jaidee had some candy to give to her five children. She first took five pieces for herself and then evenly divided the rest among her children. Each child received three pieces. With how many pieces did she start?

43) Micaela had some candy to give to her five children. She first took seven pieces for herself and then evenly divided the rest among her children. Each child received two pieces. With how many pieces did she start?

44) Ted's Bikes rents bikes for $17 plus $5 per hour. Jenny paid $57 to rent a bike. For how many hours did she rent the bike?

45) Matt bought five hats. A week later half of all his hats were destroyed in a fire. There are now only 19 hats left. With how many did he start?

46) How old am I if 500 reduced by 3 times my age is 293?

47) 444 students went on a field trip. Eight buses were filled and 20 students traveled in cars. How many students were in each bus?

48) Arjun had some paper with which to make note cards. On his way to his room he found seven more pieces to use. In his room he cut each piece of paper in half. When he was done he had 20 half-pieces of paper. With how many sheets of paper did he start?

49) Trevon wanted to make note cards by cutting pieces of paper in half. Before starting he got two more pieces to use. When he was done he had 12 half-pieces of paper. With how many pieces did he start?

50) On Tuesday Eugene bought four posters. On Wednesday half of all the posters that he had were destroyed. On Thursday there were only 22 left. How many did he have on Monday?

Answers to Chapter 9 Questions: Harder Word Problems

1) 5	2) 10	3) 3
4) 2	5) $4	6) 13
7) 14	8) 24	9) 8
10) 69	11) 22	12) 5
13) 56	14) 40	15) 9
16) 15	17) 21	18) 31
19) 7	20) 33	21) 5
22) 17	23) 5	24) 22
25) $4	26) 16	27) 23
28) 4	29) 7	30) 21
31) 25	32) 5	33) 99
34) 28	35) 8	36) 25
37) 6	38) 9	39) 24
40) $2	41) 96	42) 20
43) 17	44) 8	45) 33
46) 69	47) 53	48) 3
49) 4	50) 40	

Chapter 9 Questions: Translating Words into Equations

Write each as an algebraic expression.

1) the quotient of 24 and a

2) 3 cubed

3) the sum of n and 10

4) twice c

5) 6 less than 27

6) n squared

7) x times 6

8) 7 more than 8

9) the difference of m and 11

10) half of 20

11) the product of w and 5

12) m increased by 7

13) 18 decreased by 12

14) x cubed

15) 48 divided by 6

16) the sum of 6 and 9

17) twice 6

18) the quotient of 21 and x

19) 6 squared

20) 10 more than n

21) twice 9

22) v less than 15

23) half of 22

24) 12 times m

25) x increased by 10

26) the difference of 22 and 12

27) 48 divided by 4

28) the product of 4 and x

29) x decreased by 14

30) the quotient of n and 3

31) the sum of 4 and 6

32) 8 less than x

33) 11 times x

34) the difference of 29 and x

35) half of n

36) 12 increased by w

37) the product of v and 8

38) 23 decreased by 7

39) 24 divided by n

40) 4 cubed

41) the sum of 3 and 10

42) the quotient of 84 and x

43) 9 more than 7

44) 9 less than v

45) half of 8

46) 4 increased by 10

47) k times 9

48) the difference of 24 and p

49) x divided by 5

50) 5 cubed

Answers to Chapter 9 Questions: Translating Words into Equations

1) $\dfrac{24}{a}$
2) 3^3
3) $n + 10$
4) $2c$
5) $27 - 6$
6) n^2
7) $x \cdot 6$
8) $8 + 7$
9) $m - 11$
10) $\dfrac{20}{2}$
11) $w \cdot 5$
12) $m + 7$
13) $18 - 12$
14) x^3
15) $\dfrac{48}{6}$
16) $6 + 9$
17) $2 \cdot 6$
18) $\dfrac{21}{x}$
19) 6^2
20) $n + 10$
21) $2 \cdot 9$
22) $15 - v$
23) $\dfrac{22}{2}$
24) $12m$
25) $x + 10$
26) $22 - 12$
27) $\dfrac{48}{4}$
28) $4x$
29) $x - 14$
30) $\dfrac{n}{3}$
31) $4 + 6$
32) $x - 8$
33) $11x$
34) $29 - x$
35) $\dfrac{n}{2}$
36) $12 + w$
37) $v \cdot 8$
38) $23 - 7$
39) $\dfrac{24}{n}$
40) 4^3
41) $3 + 10$
42) $\dfrac{84}{x}$
43) $7 + 9$
44) $v - 9$
45) $\dfrac{8}{2}$
46) $4 + 10$
47) $k \cdot 9$
48) $24 - p$
49) $\dfrac{x}{5}$
50) 5^3

Chapter 9: Mixture Word Problems

1) A metal alloy weighing 9 lb. and containing 75% copper is melted and mixed with 11 lb. of a different alloy which contains 15% copper. What percent of the resulting alloy is copper?

2) For her birthday party Anjali mixed together 6 L of Brand A fruit punch and 3 L of Brand B. Brand A contains 55% fruit juice and Brand B contains 40% fruit juice. What percent of the mixture is fruit juice?

3) 20 kg of bronze was made by combining 12 kg of copper which costs $4/kg with 8 kg of tin which costs $9/kg. Find the cost per kg of the mixture.

4) 10 ft³ of soil containing 11% clay was mixed into 8 ft³ of soil containing 38% clay. What is the clay content of the mixture?

5) 12 lb of Heather's Premium Molasses was made by combining 4 lb of cane molasses which costs $1/lb with 8 lb of beet molasses which costs $4/lb. Find the cost per lb of the mixture.

6) A metal alloy weighing 7 lb. and containing 20% platinum is melted and mixed with 3 lb. of a different alloy which contains 40% platinum. What percent of the resulting alloy is platinum?

7) A metal alloy weighing 6 lb. and containing 50% gold is melted and mixed with 5 lb. of a different alloy which contains 72% gold. What percent of the resulting alloy is gold?

8) 2 yd³ of soil containing 15% clay was mixed into 1 yd³ of soil containing 30% clay. What is the clay content of the mixture?

9) 9 kg of Krystal's Premium Coffee Blend was made by combining 2 kg of arabica coffee beans which cost $4/kg with 7 kg of robusta coffee beans which cost $13/kg. Find the cost per kg of the mixture.

10) 10 lbs. of mixed nuts containing 70% peanuts were mixed with 5 lbs. of another kind of mixed nuts that contain 40% peanuts. What percent of the new mixture is peanuts?

11) 13 kg of mixed nuts containing 24% peanuts were mixed with 9 kg of another kind of mixed nuts that contain 46% peanuts. What percent of the new mixture is peanuts?

12) A metal alloy weighing 11 mg and containing 26% nickel is melted and mixed with 7 mg of a different alloy which contains 44% nickel. What percent of the resulting alloy is nickel?

13) 3 ft³ of soil containing 55% clay was mixed into 6 ft³ of soil containing 40% clay. What is the clay content of the mixture?

14) 4 m³ of soil containing 26% sand was mixed into 3 m³ of soil containing 40% sand. What is the sand content of the mixture?

15) For his birthday party Ted mixed together 9 gal. of Brand A fruit punch and 6 gal. of Brand B. Brand A contains 40% fruit juice and Brand B contains 30% fruit juice. What percent of the mixture is fruit juice?

16) 8 lbs. of mixed nuts containing 30% peanuts were mixed with 12 lbs. of another kind of mixed nuts that contain 50% peanuts. Peanuts are what percent of the new mixture?

17) A metal alloy weighing 9 kg and containing 70% copper is melted and mixed with 6 kg of a different alloy which contains 30% copper. What percent of the resulting alloy is copper?

18) 2 oz of bleached flour which costs $4/oz were combined with 1 oz of unbleached flour which costs $7/oz. Find the cost per oz of the mixture.

19) 15 kg of generic sugar was made by combining 5 kg of brand X sugar which costs $2/kg with 10 kg of brand Y sugar which costs $5/kg. Find the cost per kg of the mixture.

20) For her birthday party Chelsea mixed together 6 gal. of Brand A fruit punch and 3 gal. of Brand B. Brand A contains 20% fruit juice and Brand B contains 50% fruit juice. What percent of the mixture is fruit juice?

21) 10 lb of peanuts which cost $1/lb were combined with 5 lb of spices which cost $4/lb. Find the cost per lb of the mixture.

22) 6 oz. of mixed nuts containing 65% peanuts were mixed with 9 oz. of another kind of mixed nuts that contain 25% peanuts. Peanuts are what percent of the new mixture?

23) A metal alloy weighing 7 lb. and containing 6% iron is melted and mixed with 12 lb. of a different alloy which contains 82% iron. What percent of the resulting alloy is iron?

24) 6 oz. of mixed nuts containing 55% peanuts were mixed with 19 oz. of another kind of mixed nuts that contain 30% peanuts. Peanuts are what percent of the new mixture?

25) 8 lb of walnuts which cost $11/lb were combined with 4 lb of peanuts which cost $2/lb. Find the cost per lb of the mixture.

26) A metal alloy weighing 1 mg and containing 60% nickel is melted and mixed with 9 mg of a different alloy which contains 80% nickel. What percent of the resulting alloy is nickel?

27) A metal alloy weighing 4 lb. and containing 34% nickel is melted and mixed with 6 lb. of a different alloy which contains 84% nickel. What percent of the resulting alloy is nickel?

28) For his birthday party Arjun mixed together 10 L of Brand A fruit punch and 9 L of Brand B. Brand A contains 14% fruit juice and Brand B contains 33% fruit juice. What percent of the mixture is fruit juice?

29) A metal alloy weighing 12 lb. and containing 60% silver is melted and mixed with 8 lb. of a different alloy which contains 50% silver. What percent of the resulting alloy is silver?

30) 17 lbs. of mixed nuts containing 40% peanuts were mixed with 13 lbs. of another kind of mixed nuts that contain 70% peanuts. What percent of the new mixture is peanuts?

31) A metal alloy weighing 12 kg and containing 20% copper is melted and mixed with 8 kg of a different alloy which contains 40% copper. What percent of the resulting alloy is copper?

32) 7 kg of mixed nuts containing 30% peanuts were mixed with 5 kg of another kind of mixed nuts that contain 42% peanuts. What percent of the new mixture is peanuts?

33) 3 yd³ of soil containing 55% silt was mixed into 9 yd³ of soil containing 15% silt. What is the silt content of the mixture?

34) 9 ft³ of soil containing 50% sand was mixed into 3 ft³ of soil containing 10% sand. What is the sand content of the mixture?

35) 18 oz of premium salad mix was made by combining 6 oz of arugula which costs $3/oz with 12 oz of spinach which costs $6/oz. Find the cost per oz of the mixture.

36) 8 m³ of soil containing 25% clay was mixed into 2 m³ of soil containing 20% clay. What is the clay content of the mixture?

37) 16 kg of mixed nuts containing 60% peanuts were mixed with 4 kg of another kind of mixed nuts that contain 20% peanuts. What percent of the new mixture is peanuts?

38) For her birthday party Brenda mixed together 4 L of Brand A fruit punch and 6 L of Brand B. Brand A contains 40% fruit juice and Brand B contains 55% fruit juice. What percent of the mixture is fruit juice?

39) 3 kg of Indonesian cinnamon which costs $16/kg were combined with 9 kg of Thai cinnamon which costs $12/kg. Find the cost per kg of the mixture.

40) 6 yd³ of soil containing 20% clay was mixed into 9 yd³ of soil containing 15% clay. What is the clay content of the mixture?

41) 2 ft³ of soil containing 40% sand was mixed into 3 ft³ of soil containing 50% sand. What is the sand content of the mixture?

42) A metal alloy weighing 3 mg and containing 75% iron is melted and mixed with 7 mg of a different alloy which contains 85% iron. What percent of the resulting alloy is iron?

43) 8 oz of cane molasses which costs $1/oz were combined with 4 oz of beet molasses which costs $4/oz. Find the cost per oz of the mixture.

44) A metal alloy weighing 2 oz. and containing 30% silver is melted and mixed with 3 oz. of a different alloy which contains 60% silver. What percent of the resulting alloy is silver?

45) 3 lb of Natalie's special coffee blend was made by combining 1 lb of brand X coffee which costs $14/lb with 2 lb of brand Y coffee which costs $11/lb. Find the cost per lb of the mixture.

46) A metal alloy weighing 3 lb. and containing 50% iron is melted and mixed with 9 lb. of a different alloy which contains 90% iron. What percent of the resulting alloy is iron?

47) 4 yd³ of soil containing 54% clay was mixed into 1 yd³ of soil containing 34% clay. What is the clay content of the mixture?

48) 6 kg of mixed nuts containing 70% peanuts were mixed with 4 kg of another kind of mixed nuts that contain 60% peanuts. Peanuts are what percent of the new mixture?

49) 4 m³ of soil containing 50% clay was mixed into 6 m³ of soil containing 10% clay. What is the clay content of the mixture?

50) 4 m³ of soil containing 25% clay was mixed into 6 m³ of soil containing 20% clay. What is the clay content of the mixture?

Answers to Chapter 9: Mixture Word Problems

1) 42%
2) 50%
3) $6/kg
4) 23%
5) $3/lb
6) 26%
7) 60%
8) 20%
9) $11/kg
10) 60%
11) 33%
12) 33%
13) 45%
14) 32%
15) 36%
16) 42%
17) 54%
18) $5/oz
19) $4/kg
20) 30%
21) $2/lb
22) 41%
23) 54%
24) 36%
25) $8/lb
26) 78%
27) 64%
28) 23%
29) 56%
30) 53%
31) 28%
32) 35%
33) 25%
34) 40%
35) $5/oz
36) 24%
37) 52%
38) 49%
39) $13/kg
40) 17%
41) 46%
42) 82%
43) $2/oz
44) 48%
45) $12/lb
46) 80%
47) 50%
48) 66%
49) 26%
50) 22%

Math Practice by Kareem Gouda   www.SKOOLOO.com

Chapter 9 Questions: Scale Word Problems

Answer each question and round your answer to the nearest whole number.

1) A particular satellite is 16 m wide. A model of it was built with a scale of 1 cm : 2 m. How wide is the model?

2) A particular train is 18 ft tall. A model of it was built with a scale of 1 in : 2 ft. How tall is the model?

3) A model statue has a scale of 1 in : 5 ft. If the model statue is 2 in wide then how wide is the real statue?

4) A bird bath that is 4 ft tall casts a shadow that is 3 ft long. Find the height of an adult giraffe that casts a 12 ft shadow.

5) If a 2 ft tall lawn ornament casts a 1 ft long shadow then how tall is a baby giraffe that casts a 3 ft shadow?

6) If a 4 ft tall baby elephant casts a 1 ft long shadow then how long is the shadow that a 8 ft tall petrified stump casts?

7) A flagpole that is 16 ft tall casts a shadow that is 14 ft long. Find the length of the shadow that a 8 ft telephone booth casts.

8) A globe that is 3 ft tall casts a shadow that is 10 ft long. Find the height of a car that casts a 20 ft shadow.

9) If a 4 ft tall baby elephant casts a 2 ft long shadow then how tall is a man that casts a 3 ft shadow?

10) A ladder that is 10 ft tall casts a shadow that is 15 ft long. Find the height of a baby elephant that casts a 6 ft shadow.

11) If a 4 ft tall petrified stump casts a 6 ft long shadow then how tall is a lawn ornament that casts a 9 ft shadow?

12) A model house has a scale of 1 cm : 3 m. If the real house is 15 m wide then how wide is the model house?

13) A model igloo has a scale of 1 in : 4 ft. If the model igloo is 4 in wide then how wide is the real igloo?

14) A model car is 4 in long. If it was built with a scale of 1 in : 4 ft then how long is the real car?

15) A model building is 3 in tall. If it was built with a scale of 1 in : 6 ft then how tall is the real building?

16) If a 8 ft tall baby giraffe casts a 4 ft long shadow then how long is the shadow that a 6 ft tall man casts?

17) If a 8 ft tall baby giraffe casts a 12 ft long shadow then how tall is a tent that casts a 9 ft shadow?

18) If a 2 ft tall globe casts a 1 ft long shadow then how long is the shadow that a 6 ft tall cardboard box casts?

19) An adult giraffe that is 18 ft tall casts a shadow that is 6 ft long. Find the length of the shadow that a 3 ft car casts.

20) A statue that is 15 ft tall casts a shadow that is 3 ft long. Find the height of an adult elephant that casts a 2 ft shadow.

21) A baby elephant that is 4 ft tall casts a shadow that is 6 ft long. Find the height of a ladder that casts a 12 ft shadow.

22) A model rocket has a scale of 1 in : 3 ft. If the model rocket is 3 in tall then how tall is the real rocket?

23) A particular power plant is 12 m tall. A model of it was built with a scale of 1 cm : 3 m. How tall is the model?

24) A model house has a scale of 1 cm : 2 m. If the real house is 12 m wide then how wide is the model house?

25) A model igloo has a scale of 1 in : 6 ft. If the real igloo is 12 ft wide then how wide is the model igloo?

26) A petrified stump that is 8 ft tall casts a shadow that is 16 ft long. Find the height of a cardboard box that casts a 12 ft shadow.

27) If a 10 ft tall adult elephant casts a 5 ft long shadow then how long is the shadow that a 18 ft tall adult giraffe casts?

28) A man that is 5 ft tall casts a shadow that is 2 ft long. Find the length of the shadow that a 10 ft adult elephant casts.

29) If a 6 ft tall petrified stump casts a 18 ft long shadow then how long is the shadow that a 4 ft tall baby elephant casts?

30) A baby giraffe that is 8 ft tall casts a shadow that is 4 ft long. Find the length of the shadow that a 6 ft cardboard box casts.

31) A 10 ft tall adult elephant standing next to an adult giraffe casts a 5 ft shadow. If the adult giraffe is 14 ft tall then how long is its shadow?

32) A model car is 4 in long. If it was built with a scale of 1 in : 5 ft then how long is the real car?

33) A particular giraffe is 12 ft tall. A model of it was built with a scale of 1 in : 2 ft. How tall is the model?

34) A model rocket has a scale of 1 cm : 3 m. If the real rocket is 21 m tall then how tall is the model rocket?

35) A particular statue is 10 ft tall. A model of it was built with a scale of 1 in : 2 ft. How tall is the model?

36) A tent that is 8 ft tall casts a shadow that is 16 ft long. Find the height of an adult elephant that casts a 20 ft shadow.

37) A statue that is 18 ft tall casts a shadow that is 6 ft long. Find the length of the shadow that a 6 ft man casts.

38) If a 8 ft tall telephone booth casts a 10 ft long shadow then how tall is a baby elephant that casts a 5 ft shadow?

39) If a 20 ft tall flagpole casts a 8 ft long shadow then how tall is a tent that casts a 2 ft shadow?

40) A 6 ft tall lawn ornament standing next to a telephone booth casts a 12 ft shadow. If the telephone booth casts a shadow that is 16 ft long then how tall is it?

41) A 18 ft tall statue standing next to a petrified stump casts a 15 ft shadow. If the petrified stump casts a shadow that is 5 ft long then how tall is it?

42) A model car has a scale of 1 in : 3 ft. If the model car is 8 in long then how long is the real car?

43) If a 6 ft tall lawn ornament casts a 12 ft long shadow then how long is the shadow that a 8 ft tall cardboard box casts?

44) A model power plant is 3 in tall. If it was built with a scale of 1 in : 5 yd then how tall is the real power plant?

45) A particular car is 16 ft long. A model of it was built with a scale of 1 in : 4 ft. How long is the model?

46) A model rocket is 5 cm tall. If it was built with a scale of 1 cm : 2 m then how tall is the real rocket?

47) A model giraffe is 6 in tall. If it was built with a scale of 1 in : 3 ft then how tall is the real giraffe?

48) A 4 ft tall bird bath standing next to a globe casts a 6 ft shadow. If the globe casts a shadow that is 3 ft long then how tall is it?

49) A petrified stump that is 6 ft tall casts a shadow that is 2 ft long. Find the height of a baby elephant that casts a 1 ft shadow.

50) A 6 ft tall woman standing next to a tent casts a 2 ft shadow. If the tent casts a shadow that is 3 ft long then how tall is it?

Answers to Chapter 9 Questions: Scale Word Problems

1) 8 cm
2) 9 in
3) 10 ft
4) 16 ft
5) 6 ft
6) 2 ft
7) 7 ft
8) 6 ft
9) 6 ft
10) 4 ft
11) 6 ft
12) 5 cm
13) 16 ft
14) 16 ft
15) 18 ft
16) 3 ft
17) 6 ft
18) 3 ft
19) 1 ft
20) 10 ft
21) 8 ft
22) 9 ft
23) 4 cm
24) 6 cm
25) 2 in
26) 6 ft
27) 9 ft
28) 4 ft
29) 12 ft
30) 3 ft
31) 7 ft
32) 20 ft
33) 6 in
34) 7 cm
35) 5 in
36) 10 ft
37) 2 ft
38) 4 ft
39) 5 ft
40) 8 ft
41) 6 ft
42) 24 ft
43) 16 ft
44) 15 yd
45) 4 in
46) 10 m
47) 18 ft
48) 2 ft
49) 3 ft
50) 9 ft

Math Practice by KareemGouda   www.SKOOLOO.com

Chapter 10 Questions: Area & Circumference

Find the area of each.

1)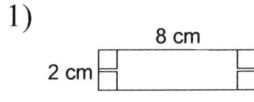

2)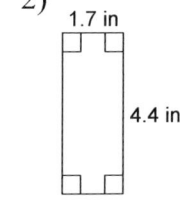

3)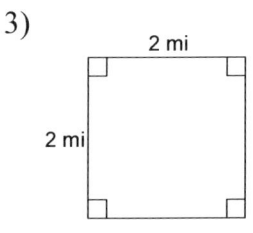

4)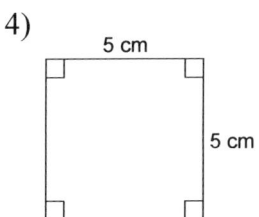

5)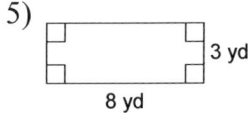

6)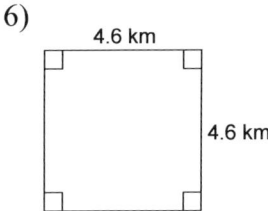

7)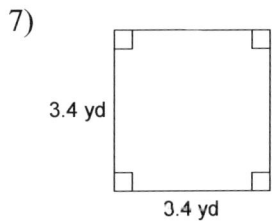

8)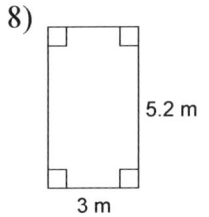

9)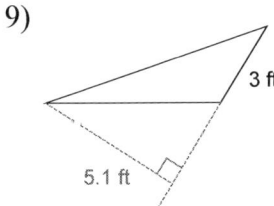

10)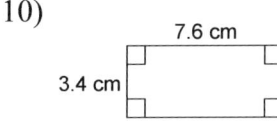

11)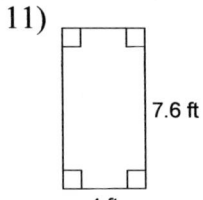

12)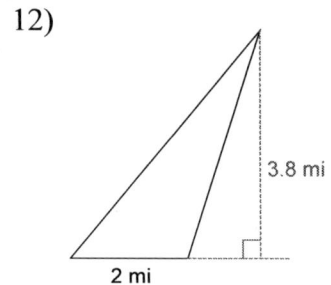

13)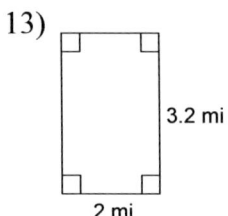

14)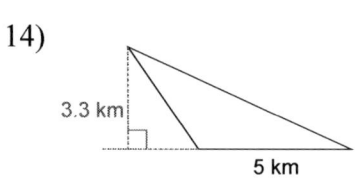

15)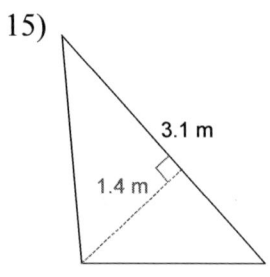

16)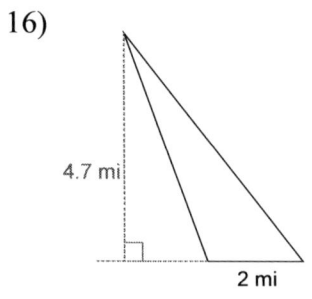

17)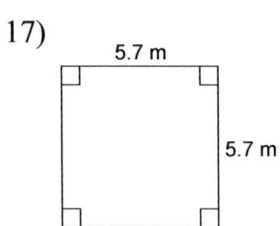

18)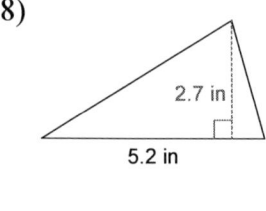

19)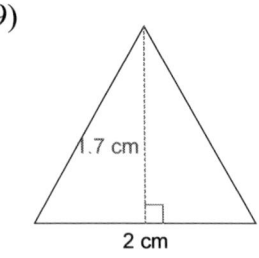

20)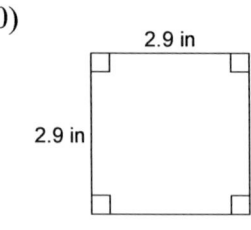

21)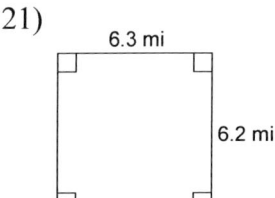

22)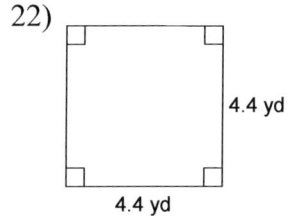

23)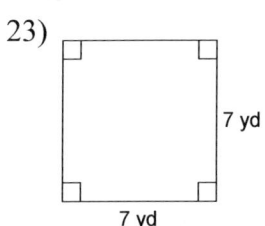

24)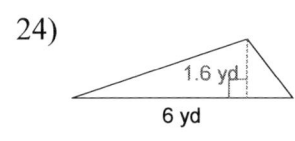

25)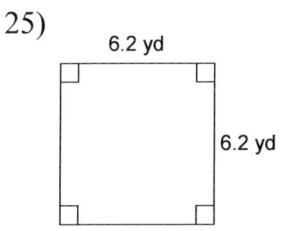

26)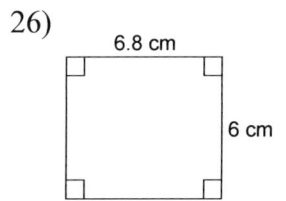

27)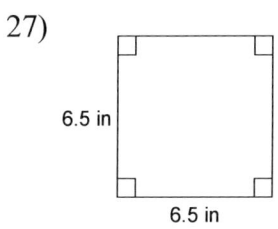

28)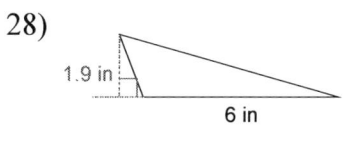

29)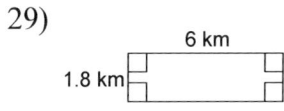

30)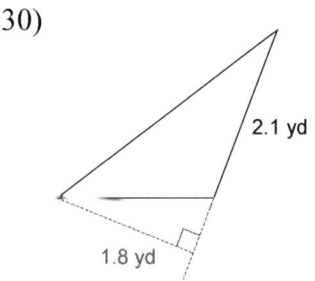

Find the area of each. Round to the nearest whole.

31)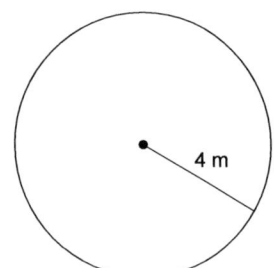

32)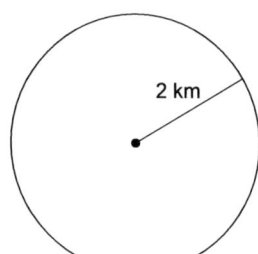

33)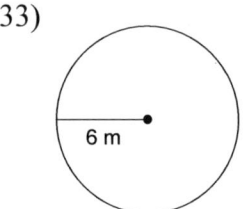

34)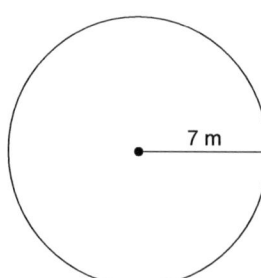

35)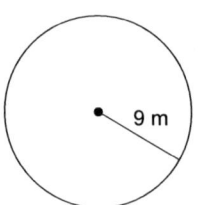

36)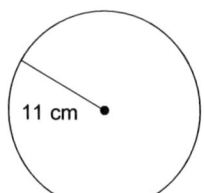

37)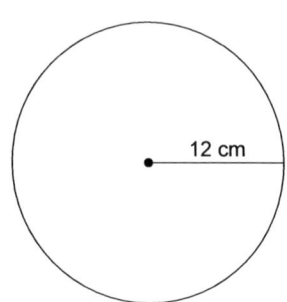

38)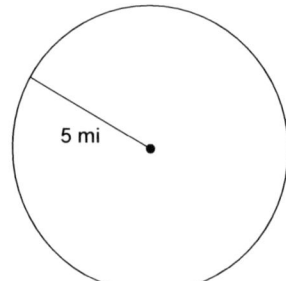

39)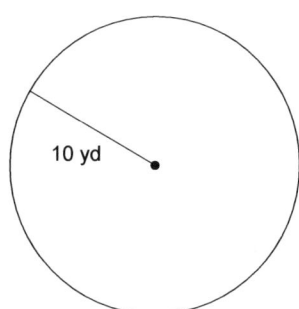

40)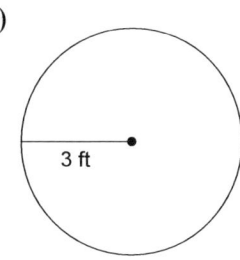

Find the circumference of each circle. Round to the nearest whole.

41)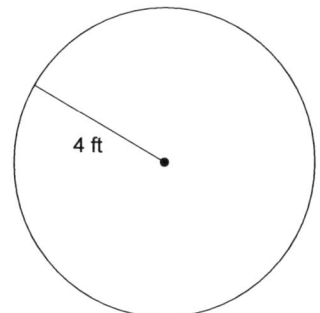

42)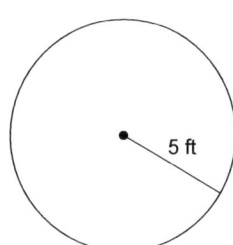

43)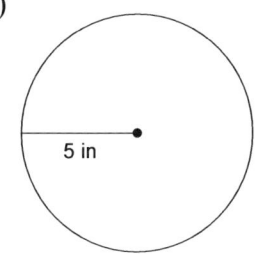

44)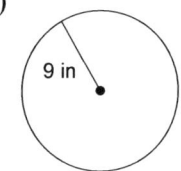

45)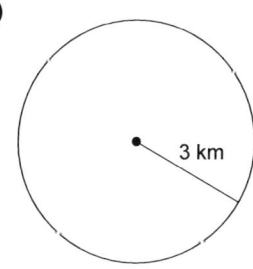

46)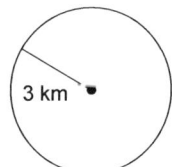

47)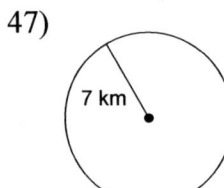

48)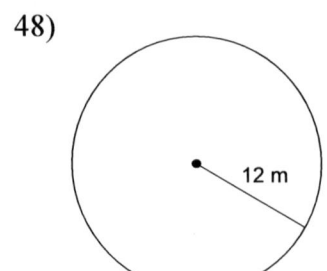

49)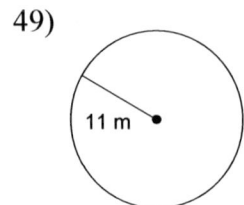

50)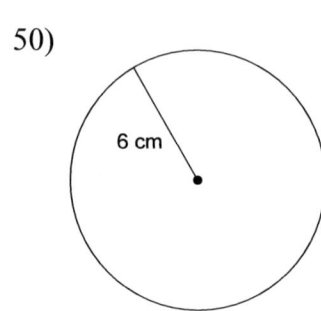

Answers to Chapter 10 Questions: Area & Circumference

1) 16 cm²
2) 7.48 in²
3) 4 mi²
4) 25 cm²
5) 24 yd²
6) 21.16 km²
7) 11.56 yd²
8) 15.6 m²
9) 7.65 ft²
10) 25.84 cm²
11) 30.4 ft²
12) 3.8 mi²
13) 6.4 mi²
14) 8.25 km²
15) 2.17 m²
16) 4.7 mi²
17) 32.49 m²
18) 7.02 in²
19) 1.7 cm²
20) 8.41 in²
21) 39.06 mi²
22) 19.36 yd²
23) 49 yd²
24) 4.8 yd²
25) 38.44 yd²
26) 40.8 cm²
27) 42.25 in²
28) 5.7 in²
29) 10.8 km²
30) 1.89 yd²
31) 50 m²
32) 13 km²
33) 113 m²
34) 154 m²
35) 254 m²
36) 380 cm²
37) 452 cm²
38) 79 mi²
39) 314 yd²
40) 28 ft²
41) 25 ft
42) 31 ft
43) 30 in
44) 57 in
45) 20 km
46) 19 km
47) 46 km
48) 72 m
49) 72 m
50) 35 cm

Made in the
USA
Middletown, DE